DATE DUE

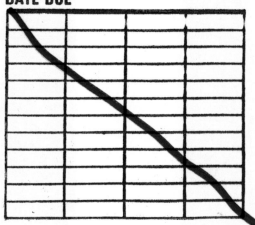

DEMCO

BASEBALL
CARDS
THE BEGINNING COLLECTOR

DAVID CRAFT

MALLARD PRESS
An imprint of
BDD Promotional Book Company, Inc.
666 Fifth Avenue
New York, New York 10103

A FRIEDMAN GROUP BOOK

Published by MALLARD PRESS
An imprint of BDD Promotional Book Company, Inc.
666 Fifth Avenue
New York, New York 10103

Mallard Press and its accompanying design and logo are trademarks of
BDD Promotional Book Company, Inc.

Copyright © 1992 by Michael Friedman Publishing Group, Inc.

First published in the United States of America in 1992 by The Mallard Press

ISBN 0-792-45477-4

THE BEGINNING COLLECTOR: BASEBALL CARDS
was prepared and produced by
Michael Friedman Publishing Group, Inc.
15 West 26th Street
New York, NY 10010

Design and Layout by: William Sponn
Photography Editor: Ede Rothaus
Photographs by: John Gruen, New York

The baseball cards and sports memorabilia in this book are from the collection and
inventory of Regal Galleries, Inc. Anyone interested in obtaining any of these
items or having questions about sports memorabilia in general may write
Regal Galleries, Inc., 101 West 57th Street, New York, New York 10019.

Typeset by: Classic Type, Inc.
Color separations by: Excel Graphic Arts Company
Printed and bound in Hong Kong by: Lee Fung-Asco Printer Ltd.

Acknowledgements

Writing this book was made simple by the knowledgeable people who served as my sources. To each and every man, woman, and child who took the time to answer a few questions, or offer a viewpoint, many thanks. You may not be quoted directly herein, but consider yourselves an important part of this book. I learned a lot from you.

Deserving of special mention here are the following, and thank you all: Donnie Tryon (and father, Dale); Bill Goodwin; Bob Lemke; Tom Mortenson; Wanda Marcus; Whitie Willenborg; Tom Owens; Rich Hawksley; and various dealers who set up at hobby shows throughout the Midwest, where some of the information for this book was gathered.

Finally, there is the matter of thanking one grandparent (still going strong at 100), and remembering the other three, for contributing to my baseball upbringing by regaling me with stories of "The Gas House Gang," the Cubs of 1908, the autographed baseball glove my dad lost, and my mom's schoolgirl crush on Phil Cavarretta. As a little kid in the 1950s and early 1960s, there was nothing better than to sit in the warmth and security of my grandparents' kitchens wolfing down a plate of homemade cookies and a glass of milk, while hearing about the old days and baseball history. Bless your hearts.

Dedication

To Karen

Who lets me store some of my baseball stuff at our home where her dollhouse miniatures might otherwise go.

CONTENTS

Introduction

*T*ime was when America's hot-stove league—baseball's off-season small talk, rumors, and reported stories—dealt almost exclusively with player trades, managerial hirings and firings, changes in team logos, and which clubs had a legitimate shot at winning the pennant.

But times have changed. The talk these days is about baseball cards: finding them, buying them, selling them, trading them, preserving them, enjoying them—collecting them.

What's more, all this talk is not restricted to the hot-stove league. It is with us throughout the year. Nor is the talk bounded by age, race, gender, or income. Granted, not everyone collects baseball cards. But sometimes it sure seems that everyone does.

Collecting baseball cards has become big business in recent years—very big business. Values of some cards rose dramatically in the 1980s, both for cards of decades past and for recently issued cards. Even baseball card–related items have hit the big time. In 1990 an uncut proof strip (of five cards circa 1910 that included legendary shortstop Honus Wagner) used to test the colors, photography, design, and paper of the cards, was going for two million dollars.

Retail shops that serve card collectors number in the thousands. Their significance to hobbyists and to the card companies themselves is so great that card shop/dealer directories are published annually.

Since 1981 there has been an increase in the number of baseball card manufacturers, too, which has resulted in a tremendous variety of card sets and related collectibles that are available to consumers. (If you desire to own one copy of every card made this year, it will cost you more than $5,000 to accomplish your goal.)

Some jaded souls see this rare 1909 tobacco card—the legendary T-206 Honus Wagner—only as an expensive investment for the very rich. (A few top-graded examples bring six-figure sums.) Other people see its beauty and simplicity and are reminded why they got into the baseball card hobby in the first place.

WAGNER, PITTSBURG

The Beginning Collector: Baseball Cards *offers the kind of basic information you'll need to get the most out of this wholesome, fascinating hobby. Along with that, you'll find the book packed with pictures of many classic baseball cards of the past one hundred years. Examples of other baseball memorabilia are inside, too. This book also includes a glossary of terms, so you'll be able to speak and understand the "language" of baseball cards. There's even a listing of major hobby publications: the various magazines, price guides, and books that have helped people just like you keep current with new products, trends, and pricing information.*

So, what are you waiting for? Enjoy The Beginning Collector: Baseball Cards, *and have fun with a hobby that will grow with you.*

—David Craft

Baseball Cards Through The Years

ADRIAN C. ANSON.
ALLEN & GINTER'S
RICHMOND. Cigarettes VIRGINIA.

SWEET
CAPORAL
CIGARETTES
The Standard
for Years

BASE BALL SERIES
350
SUBJECTS

FACTORY Nº 30, 2d 1ST. DIST. N.Y.

PASKERT, CINCINNATI.

By the time General George Armstrong Custer met his fate at the battle of Little Bighorn in 1876, the rookie card of baseball star Adrian "Cap" Anson had been out for five years.

Actually, the future Hall of Famer's debut card also featured the black-and-white portraits of his teammates on the Rockford, Illinois–based club in the National Association.

This rare *carte de visite*—what the French call a photograph mounted on cardboard—serves as a reminder that baseball cards have been with us a long, long time. In fact, even before *cartes de visite* appeared, there were tintypes (photos on tin). Later, such baseball collectibles as cabinets (usually 4″ × 6″ photos with a cardboard backing) and trade cards (similarly made, but more often used to promote a product or service than to spotlight a

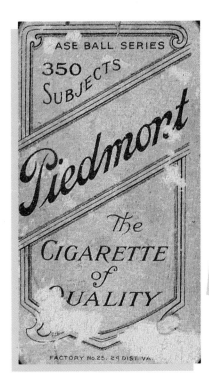

MOWREY, CINCINNATI

Tobacco cards, (left) so called because tobacco companies would package them as premiums with various brands of cigarettes, often featured the likenesses of baseball players. Because of their scarcity, many of the tobacco cards carry a hefty price tag.

His career fell between the heyday of tobacco cards and the hobby boom of the 1980s, but A.L. slugger Rudy York (below) was on cards such as those from Goudey and the Exhibit Supply Co. York, by the way, was rarely cordial to opposing pitchers. (Lifetime: 1,152 RBI: 277 HR)

player or team) were the rage.

By today's standards, some of these early entries remain quaint. That's a nice way of saying, odd or amusing. Not only did they often feature showy, ornate borders or design work, they often portrayed the players in hokey "action" poses. Shot in the studio rather than in the great outdoors—where, even in those days, the game was played—a typical photograph captured the batter "swinging" at a ball (which was suspended by a string), or the runner "sliding" into the bag (on a hardwood floor). No sweat, no dust, no reality.

Cordially
Rudy York

CIGARETTE CARDS

Mass production of baseball cards didn't really take place until about 1886 or 1887. And, while the cards them-

1887

Tobacco firms such as Goodwin & Company and Allen & Ginter begin issuing small baseball cards as premiums with their cigarettes.

selves were beautifully made, younger baseball fans of that era found that collecting them was a real challenge. Why? Because the cards were inserted in cigarette packs to serve the dual purpose of premium and package stiffener—sort of an early form of the crush-proof box.

So, while you may have experienced parental disapproval at that sugary bubble gum found in the packs of baseball cards you've collected, imagine what it must have been like back then for underage hobbyists who sought out the cards of their favorite baseball heroes. They probably hung out at the steps of their local tobacconist, asking adults who went inside if they would give them the cards from their pack of smokes. (Or worse, the kids may have handed over their allowance and asked the adults to go in and buy *them* packs of cigarettes.)

This marketing ploy was used by a number of tobacco companies during the late 1880s. One of the now-legendary card sets of that era was an issue of small ($1\frac{1}{2}'' \times 2\frac{3}{4}''$) lithographs offered by Allen and Ginter Company, of Richmond, Virginia. The backs of the cards even sported a checklist to help collectors.

Of the fifty cards in the set, only ten featured baseball players, six of whom were eventually inducted into the National Baseball Hall of Fame in Cooperstown, New York. The other forty cards in the Allen and Ginter set included sportsmen from such endeavors as boxing, rowing, and wrestling. (And perhaps as a token gesture to women, the set featured a card of famed sharpshooter Annie Oakley.)

On the heels of the Allen and Ginter issue came a *huge* set—for that time, anyway—of more than 600 player cards distributed with Old Judge brand cigarettes. This set, courtesy of the Goodwin brothers of New York City, included players not only from the National League, but also the American Association, the International League, the Pacific Coast League, the Western League, and even the Players League, which enjoyed its only season in the sun in 1890, before money woes and a lack of organiza-

Not all early baseball cards focused on "action" shots of the players. Some noted team accomplishments or sartorial splendor.

tion swamped it.

The Old Judge set was an ambitious undertaking, and many hobby historians view it as the first attempt to chronicle all of the professional players of a given period on baseball cards. The Goodwins' precursor to today's modern sets had one major flaw, however: the cards were not numbered, making it virtually impossible for collectors to acquire a complete set. Also, some players were featured—in distinct poses—on as many as a dozen cards or more.

Other tobacco companies followed suit. Either as photographs or as color lithographs, sets of varying size, design, and quality were produced and distributed periodically through the mid-1890s. In fact, some card sets from

this period are notable for their use of generic drawings. The tobacco companies employed artists to depict the players. Unfortunately, the artists had little or no idea of a given player's actual likeness. So, unless a collector knew otherwise, he or she had to assume that Joe Player in the picture really *did* have a handlebar moustache and batted left-handed.

Ironically, the formation in 1890 of the American Tobacco Company nearly spelled the demise of baseball cards. The ATC was the result of a merger of several smaller tobacco companies. Fewer companies meant less competition in the market. The need for premiums—including baseball cards—to induce people to buy their products, fell by the wayside.

Almost two decades passed before baseball cards made a comeback. And it took several Turkish tobacco firms to make it happen. Offering blends of tobacco that were new and distinctive to American taste buds, these foreign companies caused the American tobacco industry to turn over a new leaf. What's more, stateside distributors of the Turkish products offered baseball cards with packs of cigarettes sold in the United States, and that little extra set off another boom in baseball cards.

Among the more popular cards issued from 1909 to 1915 were sets from Mecca, Ramly, and Hassan, all Turkish firms. Also during this time, American candy and gum manufacturers got into the act, issuing cards with their confectionery delights—a smart move guaranteed to increase sales of candy and gum among American youngsters who couldn't get enough of sweets or baseball.

America's entry into World War I, however, caused a second major interruption in card manufacturing, as paper and printing materials were reserved for the war effort.

Although baseball itself enjoyed a renewed popularity shortly after the war ended in 1918, baseball cards and the hobby of collecting them did not, despite some unique sets issued throughout the twenties. In fact, the tobacco

> ### 1890
> Several firms merge to form the American Tobacco Company and, with less competition, baseball card premiums are virtually discontinued.

HENRY (HEINIE) MEINE

After pitching in only one game for the St. Louis Browns in 1922, Henry William Meine, known as ''The Count of Luxembourg,'' was out of the Major Leagues until 1929, when he began a successful six-year run with the Pittsburgh Pirates. During his career this card was considered common and cost pennies, but because of its age and relative scarcity, it is worth much more today.

companies quietly bowed out of the baseball card business at this time.

In their stead came companies producing everything from decks of playing cards with the hearts, clubs, diamonds, and spades surrounding photographs of big-name players to player postcards to strip cards (a continuous strip of several cards, often separated by dotted lines) to somewhat larger baseball cards on heavier stock, which were available through amusement park vending machines. These oversize cards were manufactured by Chicago's Exhibit Supply Company on up through the mid-1960s, and became known simply as Exhibit cards.

BUBBLE GUM MEETS BASEBALL

America suffered through the Dust Bowl era of the 1930s, but baseball cards enjoyed an oasis of success during the

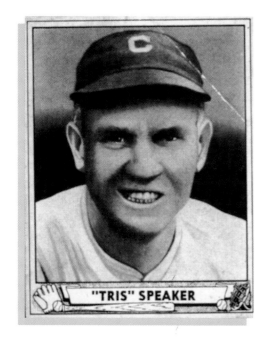

"TRIS" SPEAKER

Even years ago card manufacturers realized the need to honor former greats as well as contemporary players. This Tristram Speaker card from the classic 1940 Play Ball set recaps the Hall of Famer's career highlights on the back (opposite). On the other hand, most kids are more interested in their own generation's heroes, and Johnny Lindell, a converted outfielder with the New York Yankees, was a popular player in the 1940s. His card (left and opposite) is from the fabled 1948 Bowman set.

Great Depression with the introduction of bubble gum. In Boston, the Goudey Gum Company produced a set of base-ball cards to help market this new "food item." Goudey's 1933 and 1934 sets remain very popular with collectors today.

So do sets issued by DeLong Gum Company, National Chicle Company, and the Philadelphia-based firm of Gum, Inc., which produced a set of seventy-five cards with sepia-toned pictures of two players on each card, hence its name, the "Double Play" set.

By 1939, Gum had become the industry leader in base-ball cards, issuing such stellar sets as its 1940 "Play Ball" collection of 240 black-and-white baseball cards that remains one of the hobby's classic issues. Unfortunately for Bowman, it was hitting its stride right at the outset of U.S. involvement in World War II, when the production of baseball cards once again took a back seat to America's war effort.

Even after the war, production of baseball cards was spotty. A few regional sets, exhibit cards, and special team-issued sets were about all a collector could find until 1948, when Bowman came out with a forty-eight-card set. In each one-cent pack was a single black-and-white card and a flat piece of gum. This combination ushered in the modern era of baseball card collecting.

The new Bowmans proved so popular with collectors that the firm released a colorized (or pastel-tinted) set of 240 cards the following year. But it was Bowman's chief competitor at the time, the Leaf Gum Company, that actually introduced the first post-World War II colorized baseball cards in 1948. These cards, like the 1948 Bowmans, were considered far from the best as far as quality goes.

Leaf then issued a colorized set that purportedly featured 168 cards. In reality, there were only ninety-eight cards in the set, because their numbering was badly fouled up. Half of the ninety-eight cards in what turned out to be Leaf's last gasp in the baseball card market are relatively easy to find, the other half are not, making them among the hobby's rarest and most sought-after collectibles.

TOPPS DOMINATES THE MARKET

Bowman practically monopolized the baseball card market for the next few years. But in 1951 the Topps Company of Brooklyn, New York, which had begun as a chewing gum maker in 1938, changed all that. Topps not only issued the small set "Connie Mack All-Stars" (named in honor of the longtime Philadelphia Athletics' owner-manager), it also produced a collection of team

170. TRISTRAM E. SPEAKER
Former Major League Star
Elected to the Hall of Fame, 1937

Born: Hubbard City, Texas   August 24, 1883
Batted: Left   Threw: Left
Height: 5' 11"   Weight: 182 lbs.

Tris Speaker is one of baseball's immortals. He was perhaps the greatest defensive outfielder in baseball history, and with a lifetime batting average of .345, certainly one of its greatest hitters. Speaker played 22 years of major league ball, from 1907 through 1928, starting with the Boston Red Sox up to 1915, with Cleveland from 1916 through 1926 and with Washington and Philadelphia the next two years. He managed the Indians from 1919 until the end of 1926, and piloted Newark in the International League in 1929 and '30. Speaker still holds the doubles record in the American League with 793. Only four times in his entire career did he fail to hit .300 or better.

PLAY BALL
A pictorial news record of America's favorite sport. Save these cards . . . know all about the game and its prominent players. New pictures every year.

© 1940,   GUM, INC., Phila., Pa.   PRINTED IN U. S. A.

11 — JOHNNY LINDELL
Outfielder—N. Y. Yankees

Born: Greeley, Colo.   1916
Bats: Right   Throws: Right
Height: 6:4   Weight: 208

Joined the Yanks in 1942 as a pitcher but he developed such unusual hitting power that he was converted into an outfielder. In 1943, he led his league in triples (12). In 1944, he again led his league in triples (16). In 1945, the Army called but he was back on the team in 1946, playing first base and in the outfield. He's a policeman in California during the off-season.

ASK FOR BLONY BUBBLE GUM
The Bubble Gum with the three different flavors
BOWMAN GUM, INC. Copyright 1948

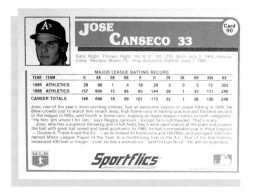

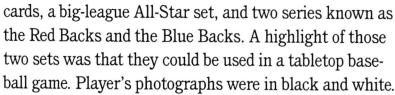

Greater care has been given to the readability of card backs in recent years. Contemporary manufacturers have enhanced the overall look of their cards with backs that boast crisp design work, full color formats, even player photos.

1909
American distributors of imported Turkish tobaccos insert cards with their products; from this, the legendary T-206 set emerges.

cards, a big-league All-Star set, and two series known as the Red Backs and the Blue Backs. A highlight of those two sets was that they could be used in a tabletop baseball game. Player's photographs were in black and white.

If Topps was shooting wildly in 1951, it hit its target in 1952 with what many collectors consider the first great card set of the modern era. With its 407 full-color cards, the 1952 Topps set included several of the game's new dynamos, such as Mickey Mantle and Willie Mays. In addition, Topp debuted its use of team logos on the front and line stats on the back of the cards. Mantle and Mays also appeared that year in the Bowman set, but those cards were, arguably, not as impressive as their Topps counterparts.

Bowman accepted the Topps challenge and issued sets through 1955, when it finally had to sell out to the overachiever from Brooklyn. As the years passed, Topps established trends that are now commonly accepted facets of baseball card production: a standard size for the cards, team logos on the card fronts, rookie cards, and cards touting league leaders in various categories (ERAs, RBIs, and so on).

Topps's position as king of the hill was never threatened in the 1960s. Leaf and Fleer made a few runs at the leader with small sets that, for Fleer anyway, also included a cookie that begged for a trip to the local bakery for the real thing.

Much like the tobacco companies generations before them, various firms in the 1950s and 1960s offered baseball cards as premiums with their products. Manufacturers of frankfurters, potato chips, and breakfast cereals regularly packaged cards with their products. In the case of Post Cereals in the early 1960s, the cards *were* the package. (Or at least, the back panels of selected cereal boxes were, if one carefully trimmed along the borders separating the individual cards.)

But Topps continued its domination of the market until 1981, when the company lost a lawsuit that paved the

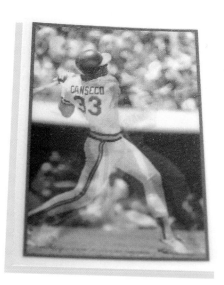

Baseball card technology has changed dramatically since the days of photographing a stationary batter ''swinging'' at a baseball suspended by a string. Sportflics, with its distinctive ''Magic Motion'' cards, uses three-dimensional images (these three images are from one card) to convey a sense of movement in the player's form. Sportflics was the first company to print entire sets using a multi-image design.

way for others to produce baseball card sets for national distribution. Fleer, and then Donruss of Memphis, Tennessee, began producing cards with bubble gum. While the courts later ruled that only Topps could offer gum products with its cards, the competitive card market was just starting to heat up.

In 1986, the Sportflics brand of baseball cards hit the hobby world with an exclusive process that produced three-dimensional images on a single card. Called ''Magic Motion'' cards, they showed a batter taking a swing at the plate, or a pitcher firing the ball homeward.

Two years later, collectors had the opportunity to buy Score cards from the same company that produces Sportflics (Major League Marketing and Optigraphics). Score cards feature full-color backs.

Upper Deck issued its first sets in 1989. Manufactured by a California company, Upper Deck cards are specially coated to reduce damage from normal handling and moisture.

THE FUTURE OF THE HOBBY

"The future," longtime relief ace Dan Quisenberry once said, "is much like the present, only longer." Those words of wisdom could apply to the hobby of collecting baseball cards as easily as they do to life in general.

Think of the number and variety of cards that have been issued since the American Civil War—a period of less than 150 years. Look at the innovations that have taken place in the hobby in just the last few years. Now, try to imagine what might lie in store for collectors over the next 150 years.

No wonder people of all ages get excited about a hobby that continues to surprise and delight—just like baseball itself.

STARTING YOUR COLLECTION

LOU BO

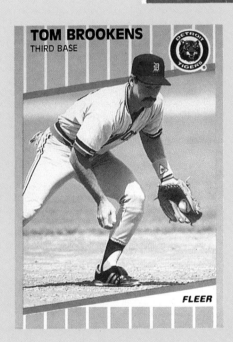

TOM BROOKENS
THIRD BASE

FLEER

OUTFIELD
BRAVES

HANK
AARON

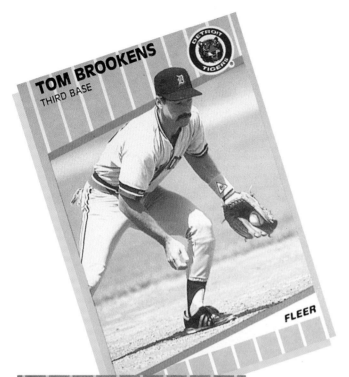

Every effort is made to catch errors before a card is printed. Still, accidents do happen. Can you spot the major error shared by this Tom Brookens card and the Mike Heath on page 25?

TOM BROOKENS
THIRD BASE

FLEER

FLEER 130	MIKE HEATH
	TIGERS • CATCHER

Height 5'11", Weight 180, Bats Right, Throws Right
Born 2-5-55, Tampa, FL
Home Brandon, FL

Yr. Club	Pct.	G	AB	R	H	2B	3B	HR	RBI	SB	BB	SO
73 John Cty	.175	48	166	17	29	5	2	0	10	7	13	37
74 Oneonta	.282	65	234	51	66	6	3	3	34	6	28	34
75 Ft Laudr	.231	98	376	43	87	7	3	1	23	13	25	50
76 Ft Laudr	.266	80	267	28	71	16	3	2	30	0	13	43
77 W Haven	.267	98	352	58	94	13	5	8	42	5	29	55
78 Yankees	.228	33	92	6	21	3	1	0	8	0	4	9
79 Tucson	.270	54	196	21	53	8	2	1	28	2	16	25
79 A's	.256	74	258	19	66	8	0	3	27	1	17	18
80 A's	.243	92	305	27	74	10	2	1	33	3	16	28
81 A's	.236	84	301	26	71	7	1	8	30	3	13	36
82 A's	.242	101	318	43	77	18	4	3	39	8	27	36
83 A's	.281	96	345	45	97	17	0	6	33	3	18	59
84 A's	.248	140	475	49	118	21	5	13	64	7	26	72
85 A's	.250	138	436	71	109	18	6	13	55	7	41	63
86 Cards	.205	65	190	19	39	8	1	4	25	2	23	36
86 Tigers	.265	30	98	11	26	3	0	4	11	4	4	17
87 Tigers	.281	93	270	34	76	16	0	8	33	1	21	42
88 Tigers	.247	86	219	24	54	7	2	5	18	1	18	32
ML Totals	.250	1032	3307	374	828	136	22	68	376	40	228	448

BEFORE	THE ALL STAR BREAK	**AFTER**
BATTING AVG. .256		BATTING AVG. .235
HOME RUNS 4		HOME RUNS 1
RBI 13		RBI 5

© 1989 FLEER CORP. PHILA. 19141   PRINTED IN U.S.A.

*T*here are two things you should know before you start collecting baseball cards: (1) you can't collect 'em all and (2) you must set goals.

Reality will take care of the first point. By themselves, the new sets issued each year—major (national) sets and their corresponding update sets, as well as regional sets, food sets, and all the others—total more than 200. Add to that figure the thousands of card sets and individual cards dating back to the late 1800s that are still available in limited quantity, and you can understand the need for planning ahead.

Spending limits and your own particular interests will take care of the second point. Do you want to spend 50¢ or $50 a year on cards? As much as $100 or more? Is it a particular set you want to own, or five mint-condition

Collectors discovered a bonus when they realized that Fleer made a mistake when it issued its 1989 set: The stats for Tiger teammates Tom Brookens and Mike Heath were transposed. The company later issued corrected cards numbered 130b and 132b, respectively. An ''error'' card is sometimes worth more than the corrected version if it is less common than its replacement.

cards of this season's hottest rookie star? It's up to you.

This chapter will offer some guidelines to help you narrow your decisions and have fun with the hobby. It will even give a few money-saving tips along the way. But the key word here is "fun," which is what collecting baseball cards is really all about.

SEVERAL OPTIONS

For sheer value, your best bet is to buy a current, complete set of cards all at once, preferably one collated (assembled numerically) and packaged by the card company itself. This is called a "factory set." Granted, this may not be as exciting as opening a sealed wax pack to discover what it holds among its fifteen or so cards, but buying a current factory set issued by one of the major

card companies eliminates the need for buying dozens of those individual wax packs (or cello packs or rack packs) in order to assemble a complete set.

Initially, it may cost you more to purchase a current factory set from one company—$20 to $45 total to buy a set —than it would to buy a few individual packs of cards to start your collection. "But with today's poor collation," says longtime collector Tom Owens, of Gig Harbor, Washington, "there's no guarantee that you can put together a complete set out of one or two boxes of wax packs." (Typically, there are thirty-six wax packs in each wax box.)

"Sometimes, collectors can't be sure whether individual packages of cards have been tampered with, unless they buy factory-sealed boxes of wax packs. So, if you're talking strictly value, then complete sets are your best buy. If the collector does purchase a complete set, I guess I would recommend Topps, first of all, because that company has the best track record when it comes to value appreciation," adds Owens.

Donnie Tryon, veteran hobbyist and part owner of his family's card shop in Ames, Iowa, agrees that the best way to go is to buy a whole set. "By buying a current, complete set, you're getting hundreds of 'commons'— cards of players who are average to good, but not the superstars like Jose Canseco or Don Mattingly," Tryon points out. "But you're also going to *get* those superstar cards plus a few rookie cards that may increase in value over time, and those cards will help maintain the set's value."

But what if your card-buying budget won't stretch to $20 or more?

"Then I would go with just buying a few wax packs at 40¢ or 50¢ apiece," Tryon says. "That will at least give the beginning collector the thrill of opening the wrappers and seeing what's inside. Who knows? Maybe some superstar cards or cards of a few hot rookie prospects will be inside.

"Or, the beginning collector might want to buy a team set if he or she has a favorite team. That's another good way—an inexpensive way—to start your collection," says Tryon. Indeed, team sets assembled from a current factory set are one of the more popular means of collecting these days. An example of a team set would be the 1990 Fleer cards of Howard Johnson, Kevin McReynolds, Dwight Gooden, Darryl Strawberry, and the other Mets who are featured on individual cards in Fleer's 1990 set. Another example would be the individual cards of all the Red Sox players featured in the 1967 Topps set, including those of Carl Yastrzemski and Jim Lonborg.

As a beginning collector, you can either assemble your team set gradually, through the purchase of wax packs or single cards, or buy a prepackaged team set at almost any major retailer or discount store. "A team set," Tryon adds,

Players who are traded after a company's annual major card set is issued are among those included in "updated" or "traded" card sets. They are pictured in the uniforms of their new teams. Also offered in these smaller sets are rookies that weren't included in the major set. Updated/ traded sets are a fairly recent addition to the hobby.

1917
America's entry into World War I causes a shortage of paper and ink products, effectively stopping production of baseball cards.

Hammer time: When this 1968 Topp's card of baseball's career home run leader was issued, Henry "Hammerin' Hank" Aaron still had more than 270 home runs left in his swing. Even in only very good condition, this card brings as much as twelve dollars. Note that the card front features a background reminiscent of burlap. For Aaron, particularly, that seems appropriate; potatoes are shipped in burlap and Hank hit a lot of "taters."

1921
Exhibit Supply Company of Chicago issues cards of celebrities, including ballplayers, at penny arcades and amusement parks.

"is as good a place to start collecting as any."

Another relatively inexpensive and easy collection to put together involves individual players. Say, for example, you're a big fan of Major Leaguer Bobby Bonilla, who debuted in 1986. Why not assemble a collection of all of his cards—such as every Topps card of him issued thus far, or every card of him issued by *all* the major companies, including Topps, Fleer, Score, Donruss, and Upper Deck? Throw in his Sportflics "Magic Motion" cards for good measure, and you've got quite a collection showing your support for your favorite player.

Or, consider collecting the cards of players on last-place teams. That may sound funny, but collecting is supposed to be fun. Besides, some of the memories that baseball fans hold so dear encompass the exploits of cellar dwellers like the 1962 Mets or the 1969 Seattle Pilots.

ROOKIE CARDS

Much of what you hear about collecting involves cards of rookie players. Not a season goes by without one or more young "phenoms" creating some excitement with their accomplishments on the field, and not a season goes by without a lot of talk about whether their rookie cards will be good investments.

These talented newcomers embark on what they hope will be long and successful careers. Some make the big leagues to stay. Others, as the saying goes, manage to stay just long enough for a cup of coffee. And as the player goes, so goes his card. Some rookie cards will appreciate in value, while the values of other rookie cards will drop so fast you'll wonder what all the excitement was about in the first place. But even if the player flops, his rookie card will likely remain as his most popular among collectors.

Investing in current rookie cards has been a boon to the hobby. It has stimulated interest (and sales) in baseball cards in general. In fact, the demand for rookie cards has become so great that in recent years some collectors began looking to minor league sets to find pre-rookie cards of some players. (And at least one dealer was offering copies of Don Mattingly's high school yearbook, showing the superstar's class photograph in the advertisement.) Baby pictures, anyone?

Because the card companies begin issuing their new, complete sets in January or February of each year, company officials must make certain decisions about which players to include in their sets. These decisions, of course, are made before many of the trades are announced by the Major League teams, and before some of the up-and-coming rookies are placed on the Major League rosters. Some rookies do wind up in these sets, however.

That is why you see updated/traded card sets issued in the fall. These smaller sets (about one-fifth the number of cards found in a regular set) reflect all the changes that took place *after* the companies' self-imposed mid-winter deadline: notable rookies and other players who were not included in the regular set, plus the traded players pictured in the uniforms of their new teams.

In the hobby world there is a subtle difference between a player's rookie card and his first card. Knowing the difference is important: Most dealers and collectors consider a player's rookie card to be the first *regular-issue* card from one of the major card manufacturers that shows the player in a big-league uniform. Cards of new faces found in ''updated'' or ''traded'' sets are *not* considered true rookie cards by most collectors because the sets themselves are sold almost exclusively through card shops and hobby dealers and not to the general public at local grocery stores, convenience shops, and the like.

Here's an example: Slugger Will Clark first appeared on a Major League card in Fleer's 1986 Update set. But the hobby considers Clark's *rookie* card to be the one that appeared the following year, in Fleer's 1987 regular set of 660 cards. Just remember, most people in the hobby view a player's rookie card as the one that shows him in a Major League uniform in a company's *regular set*, whether

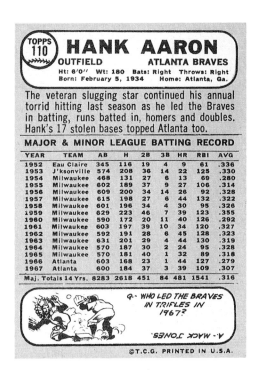

it's by Fleer, Topps, Score, or any of the other leading card makers. (In some cases, a player's rookie card also happens to be his first card—but not always.)

Concentrating on rookie cards is much like buying "penny stocks" on Wall Street. It's pure speculation whether a particular newcomer will go on to have a Hall of Fame–type career, thereby increasing the value of his rookie card. As one veteran "rookie watcher" wistfully puts it, "For every Jose Canseco there is a Joe Charboneau."

If you want to speculate on rookie cards in hopes of turning a profit at a later time, there are a few things to keep in mind. First, buy only mint-condition rookie cards and store them in a safe, temperature-controlled place. Anyone interested in purchasing them from you will scoot out your door if the cards are damaged in any way.

Second, do your homework. Read up on these fresh faces, know who they are, and try to determine their potential in the big leagues by studying their numbers in the minors. Newspapers and magazines are a good way to keep track of minor league players, through box scores, game recaps, and player profiles. And don't forget live radio and TV coverage of ballgames.

Third, consider buying rookie cards in lots of twenty-five or more, as you will pay less per card this way than if you buy just two or three of each player.

Fourth, watch to see what rookie cards most speculators are buying, and then consider going after other rookie cards. Not only will you save some money, since a strong demand for certain cards will jack their prices up considerably, but you may find a hidden gem among the rookie cards that few other speculators managed to spot.

Finally, it's best to steer clear of pitching prospects, no matter how nasty their curveball is or how small their fastball appears to opposing batters. No player is immune from injury, but too many things can go wrong with a pitcher's throwing arm to warrant an investment of your hard-earned bucks on rookie mound aces. If you have to

Future Hall of Famer Lou Boudreau was in select company when he appeared in Leaf's 1948–49 set. His was the 53rd card in a 98-card-set. How can that be, you ask, if his card is numbered 106? The company, for some strange reason, skip-numbered its cards between 1–186. Go figure. (But don't laugh too long: A complete set in near-mint condition will cost about fifteen grand.)

have a Dennis Eckersley or a Roger Clemens rookie card, that's fine. But do concentrate on nonpitchers.

ERROR CARDS AND VARIATIONS

"To err is human," wrote English poet Alexander Pope, to which a collector might add, "but there is no guarantee of profit from it."

Within the hobby of baseball card collecting, it's a "given" that each new season will bring a few cards containing one or more errors. A misspelled name, an incorrect photograph, the wrong position listed for the player, and bogus stats are all common goofs. Even an obscenity on the player's bat, such as those found on the notorious 1989 Fleer card of Billy Ripken or the only slightly less

106---LOU BOUDREAU
Shortstop—Cleveland Indians

Age—32	Bats—right
Ht.—5′ 11″	Throws—left
Home—Harvey, Ill.	Wgt.—170 lbs.

"Most valuable player" in 1948. Only player-manager. Paced Indians to world's championship last season with .355 bat mark (2nd best to Ted Williams, the leader) and led shortstops in fielding with .975. Batted .263 in World Series vs. Boston. Set new fielding mark for infielders in 1947 with .982 average. Won bat title in 1944 with .327.

ALL-STAR BASEBALL GUM

Collect this series of Diamond Greats

Decorate your room with colorful felt pennants of your favorite teams. Send 5 All-Star Baseball Wrappers and 10c for big 12″ x 6″ pennant of any team in the American league or the National league.

Send Wrappers and Coin to
LEAF GUM CO., Box 5907 CHICAGO 80, ILL.
Copyright 1948

offensive Jim Nettles card in the 1990 "Senior Professional Baseball" set from Pacific Trading Company, does occur from time to time.

And sometimes, just as he is on the playing field, it is the player himself who is responsible for the error on his card. Righthander Lew Burdette, once a mainstay of the Braves when they were simply Milwaukee's team, decided he wanted to appear on his 1959 Topps card as a southpaw.

Another "card" on his card was former catcher Bob Uecker, who pulled a similar righty-lefty switch on the photographer. Uecker, who once played the tuba in the outfield prior to a World Series game, is pictured on his 1965 Topps card as a left-handed hitter for St. Louis. (Considering Ueck's lifetime .200 batting average, perhaps he should have pursued that batting switch.)

Are these error cards worth anything? Sometimes. If the error is never corrected by the card manufacturer, then the card takes on no additional value. If the manufacturer does issue a second version of the card—called a "variation"—then the error card *may* be worth more than its replacement. There have even been instances of several variations of the same card. Generally speaking, the version that will (over the long haul) have the greatest value will be the one that is least common, and it takes time for the market to figure out which card fits that description.

Buying error cards in lots of twenty-five to one hundred as potential money-makers is, like rookie card purchases, pure speculation. Some hobbyists give it a try, others do not. But at the very least, error cards are fun to own, look at, and discuss with fellow collectors. They always make great conversation pieces and add much to baseball card lore.

MINOR LEAGUE SETS

As the rookie card craze continued into the 1990s, minor league sets were being considered as possible investment

---

1933
Goudey, followed by National Chicle, DeLong, and others, markets baseball cards with slabs of a new "food item"—bubble gum.

opportunities. Some dealers, especially, view these sets as having a current major league star's true rookie card, and will advertise them as such.

Will minor league sets really be valuable as the years go by? The jury, it seems, is still out. They have yet to gain a universal following that mirrors the popularity of Major Leaguers' cards.

What is known is this: more than one hundred minor league card sets are currently being produced, with press runs ranging from about 4,000 to 10,000 sets each. Obviously, that means there are limited quantities out there for collectors. Yet, despite this, the country's network of collectors and dealers has made it a little easier for, say, someone in California, to obtain a set of cards depicting members of the Yankees' farm club in Albany, New York.

Minor league sets usually start at about $5 or $6. But if some current Major League player—a Rickey Henderson, a Roger Clemens, or a Bo Jackson—is featured in a particular minor league set, figure on shelling out more money for it than you would for a minor league set containing no "marquee names."

Many collectors simply enjoy owning all the sets of their favorite big league team's minor league franchises. Some collectors, regardless of whom they root for at the Major League level, obtain the yearly sets of the minor league team closest to where they live, to show support for the "local nine"—and to add to their collections.

REPRINT SETS

Reproductions of previously issued (and out-of-print) card sets have been with us for years. Though of little intrinsic value because they're not the originals, these sets do serve a useful purpose. They enable collectors of all ages to own some of the classic, even legendary, baseball cards of all time for bargain prices.

A casual glance at selected ads in the hobby publications will tell you that for about $5 you can obtain a reprint set of twenty Old Judge brand tobacco cards from

Polar Bear
IS NOW
ALWAYS HAS BEEN
ALWAYS WILL BE
The Best
Scrap Tobacco.

BASE BALL SERIES
Assorted Designs

C.C.C. Reprint—1988

Reprints lack the value of the originals, but they allow avid collectors the opportunity to own vintage baseball cards for a fraction of the cost of the originals. Think of them as history in the remaking. (The original is on the opposite, the reprint is above.)

1880. For $10 or so you can get one hundred Goudey cards first issued in 1934. And if you really want to splurge, the historic 1940 black-and-white "Play Ball" series containing 240 cards is yours for a mere $25. Even the granddaddy of all baseball cards, the Honus Wagner T-206 tobacco card, is among the 524 cards in a reprint set that retails for about $40. Not bad when you consider that the estimable shortstop's actual T-206 in top condition goes for five- and six-figure sums.

So, while reprint sets aren't valuable in and of themselves, collectors with an interest in the history of baseball cards would do well to consider adding one or more of them to their collections.

As a beginning collector, don't be overwhelmed by what's out there. Think of yourself as an explorer who, after carefully charting your course, is on the verge of discovering something wonderful in a new land you've only heard about.

Baseball cards may be just pieces of cardboard with pictures on them, but they are the undisputed gems of the baseball hobby world. Acquiring them, learning about their varieties, talking about them with your friends and family, and assembling them in your own unique collection will provide a lifetime of enjoyment.

And remember: decide what you want to collect, then go for it.

STORING AND DISPLAYING YOUR CARDS

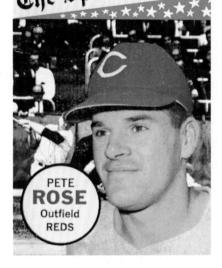

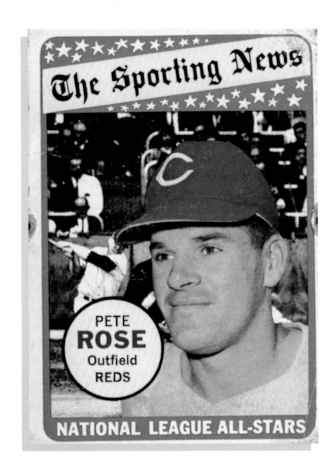

Teammates band together, baseball cards don't. At least, not if the collector cares about the condition of the cards. Holding cards with a rubber band causes "notching," one of the surest ways to ruin their appearance and decrease their value.

Repeat this to yourself five or six times: "I will not loop rubber bands around my baseball cards."

Finished? Good. You're already on your way to caring for your cardboard treasures properly. Baseball cards should never, ever, be bound by rubber bands. Doing so will cause *notching*—the term the hobby world uses to describe the indentations along a card's edge. And notching is a sure way to decrease the value of a card and destroy its beauty. Even if you don't plan to sell your cards, wouldn't you rather have them in tiptop shape years from now than have them old and creased?

There are other pitfalls to avoid when storing your cards, too:

• Don't pack your cards into a container as if they were

sardines.

- Don't store cards loosely in a box, allowing them to "knock about."
- Don't store cards in excessively cold or hot areas.
- Don't leave cards in damp areas such as laundry rooms or garages.
- Don't leave cards in areas of bright sunlight, causing them to fade.
- Don't handle cards if your hands are greasy, sticky, or ink-smeared.
- Don't store cards where small children can reach them.
- Don't use any type of device (tweezers, hemostat) to pick up cards.
- Don't handle your cards excessively, thus increasing chances of mishaps.

Three-ring binders may be a reminder of schooldays past, but they also serve as a tried-and-true method for storing baseball cards. Collectors and dealers alike use them. Take care when sliding the cards into their pocketed sheets, and store the binders in temperature-controlled places, out of reach of small children and pets.

OK, now for the dos. You've got several good options for storing and preserving your baseball cards. What you choose to do depends largely on whether you want to display your cards and have easy access to them or keep them tucked away. It's a very personal choice.

Let's say you want to care for them safely but still be able to look at them or show them to your friends from time to time.

For that, you will need to buy three-ring binders (notebooks) and corresponding vinyl, pocketed sheets in which to store your cards. Your local hobby shop should carry both, although if you prefer binders stamped with a particular logo (school emblem, TV cartoon character, funny slogan) you can probably find them at selected retail stores in your area that carry school supplies.

The three-ring vinyl, pocketed sheets, however, are another matter. They are designed specifically for baseball cards. What's more, manufacturers offer collectors a variety of sheet styles to accommodate specific card sizes.

The older, smaller tobacco cards, for instance, take sixteen-pocket sheets; Topps cards issued prior to 1957 take one size of sheet, while Topps cards issued from 1957 to the present take another size of sheet; and so on. There are more than a dozen different sheet styles and sizes and several sheet manufacturers, so talk to your dealer about what's best for your collection. In any case, don't skimp on the quality. If your cards are treasures to you, treat them as such.

Also, there are sheets for loading your cards from the top, which is the easier, preferred method, and side-loading sheets. Try to get sheets with prepunched holes in them for easy use. (Always make sure the holes are punched clean through *before* you insert your cards into the sheets. Otherwise, you may damage your cards if you try to force the sheets onto the rings.)

As for the binders themselves, ideally you'll want to place about sixty sheets of cards in each notebook, but

---

1939
Gum begins issuing its yearly sets of "Play Ball" cards; the 1940 set eventually gains status as a hobby classic.

Cards of different sizes take pocketed, vinyl sheets of different sizes. A tobacco card of decades ago requires a 16-pocket sheet, while most of today's cards will fit nicely into vinyl sheets designed specifically for modern issues. There are several sizes of sheets made by various firms using different materials. Discuss all your storage needs with your dealer.

you can put in as many as eighty or ninety without causing a "stress fracture" in your notebook.

Veteran collector and retailer Donnie Tryon emphasizes that collectors should store their notebooks in temperature-controlled places. "Keeping your cards in notebooks is fine if (collectors) want to flip the pages back and forth without damaging the cards," Tryon says, "but the notebooks themselves should be stored in temperature-controlled settings.

"Cards can pretty much last forever in the notebooks if they're properly handled, but I've seen several instances where someone has left a notebook in the back of the car, and the heat from the sun has melted the plastic all over the cards. Notebooks shouldn't be left in the car during *any* time of the year," cautions Tryon.

JEFFERSON R. BURDICK AND THE AMERICAN CARD CATALOGUE

*S*yracuse, New York, has always been a good baseball town—so perhaps it's not too surprising that it was the home of Jefferson R. Burdick, the man credited with being "the father of modern card collecting."

Burdick's enormous collection of tobacco cards, trade cards, postcards, and other paper mementos depicted not only baseball heroes, but film stars, flags of the world, and many other subjects. During the 1940s, he keyed the development of *The American Card Catalogue* (ACC), first published in 1960.

This essential work classifies cards by year and type, not by the manufacturer's name. For exam-ple, the designation "T" stands for "Twentieth Century U.S. tobacco" card. Likewise, an "N" before a given number tells the collector that the card is a "Nineteenth Century U.S. tobacco" card. An "E" stands for "early candy and gum" card. An "F" signifies a "food insert" card, and so on.

Burdick, who died in 1963, donated his mammoth collection of cards to the Metropolitan Museum of Art in New York City. It can be seen by appointment only. The one drawback to this particular exhibit is that visitors cannot see the backs of the cards—Burdick pasted his tiny treasures into scrapbooks to deter thieves.

Whether you leave your cards in their original container or place them in a substitute carton, always make sure they are stored properly (opposite, top). A number of dealers around the country offer a selection of sturdy boxes with different storage capacities. Who knows what this Mark Gardner card will be worth in a few years if it is kept in good condition?

BOXES

Many collectors, notably those intending to sell their cards at a profit at some future date, store their cards in such a way that damage control overrides their desire to display the cards. Of course, if you have a factory set, then the cards already come in their own custom-fitted container. You buy the set and put it away; it's that simple.

On the other hand, if you hand-collate a set from wax packs or other configuration before storing it, you should try to get specially designed cardboard boxes—known collectively as "dealer boxes"—to store your cards. Once you've figured out how many cards you have and the amount of space you'll need to store them, talk with your dealer to learn what size of box best suits your needs.

Even shoe boxes or other cardboard containers that may be lying about the house can be used to store your cards. But you need to prevent the cards from knocking about inside the box. Here's how:

1. Place the cards on their sides inside the box and gently push them squarely against one end of the box.

2. Stuff a clean, dry, preferably soft, cloth such as an old (white) T-shirt inside the box at the other end of the row of cards; if there is space on either side of the row, stuff additional material there to prevent shifting inside the box; don't use old cleaning rags, which may contain harmful residues.

3. Replace the box lid and store the box in a cool (not cold), dry, dark place for safekeeping; you may wish to fasten the lid gently to the outside of the box with tape.

4. Do not stack the boxes.

STORING INDIVIDUAL CARDS

Maybe you have a special card that you'd like to put on display, yet you still don't want to risk damaging it. You have a couple of options. One method is to insert your card carefully into a single-card vinyl holder, sometimes called a card-gards. You'll still want to follow all the standard storage rules (cool, dry, dark place, and so on), but at least you can pick the card up and look at it without actually touching its surface. A single-card holder resembles one pocket of a larger vinyl sheet, and usually costs no more than a quarter. Some card-gards are more rigid than others, so buy to suit your needs.

A second method of spotlighting that special card of yours is to slip it into a free-standing, acrylic holder. However, these display devices are not airtight, so you should not keep the card this way over a long period time. There is a danger of accidentally spilling a beverage into the opening or knocking the holder over and sending the card flying out of its slot.

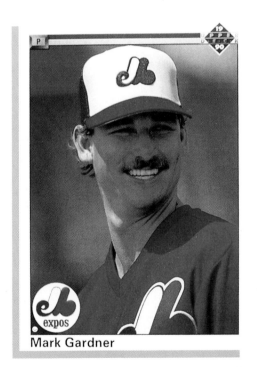

Mark Gardner

Dealers and collectors alike often display their most prized cards in what's called a deluxe case. A deluxe case consists of two sections of clear, rigid plastic that fit tightly over the entire card to allow frequent handling without fear of damaging the card. Some cases snap together, others are fastened at the corners by screws.

Some collectors display both a card of their favorite player and an autographed baseball in a specially designed holder on a wood base.

Check out the ads in the hobby publications. New products to help you preserve your cards, as well as variations on existing products, are coming out all the time. There are even sturdy storage and display boxes, actually called shoe boxes, that are available to you. They can hold hundreds or even thousands of cards.

Finally, experience helps. Talk with reputable dealers and a few veteran collectors. Find out what they use to protect their prized baseball cards.

Buying, Selling, And Trading Your Cards

John Franco — PITCHER

RICO PETROCELLI — Shortstop

RED SOX

Coinciding with the tremendous growth in baseball card collecting during the 1980s were the thousands of retail card shops that sprang up all across the United States. These days, larger, metropolitan areas of the country may boast a dozen or more such shops, but even medium-size communities and small towns will be likely to have one or two.

Some of these businesses actually began as shops specializing in coins, antiques, or some other type of collectible. But when the boom hit the baseball card market in the mid-1980s, many store owners saw the need to diversify their inventory, sometimes switching completely to cards. It's safe to say that few of these retailers have come to regret their decisions.

The dramatic rise in the popularity of baseball cards in the 1980s coincided with a similar boom in the number of fans going through the turnstiles at Major League ballparks. Kirby Pucket's enthusiastic style of playing mirrors the enthusiasm in the hobby.

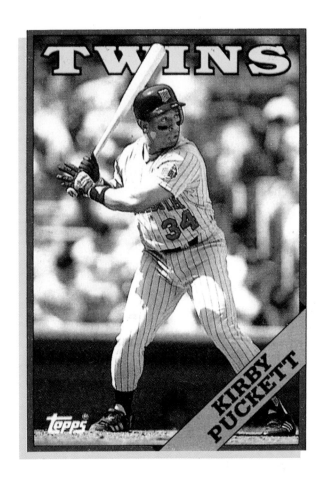

Card shops have established themselves as the backbone of the hobby. Typical locations will feature everything from the latest factory sets to single cards of yesterday's heroes; hobby publications to current price guides in paperback; storage devices such as vinyl sheets and plastic stands to autographed 8 × 10 glossies of Hall of Famers.

If you want to be treated fairly and with respect by the dealer, it's a good idea to have a basic understanding of the hobby *before* you step inside the store. Start with this book. You don't have to memorize every term in the glossary provided here (pages 99 to 117), but you should know the names of the major card manufacturers and some of their history, as well as some of the basics of grading, storage, and types of cards on the market.

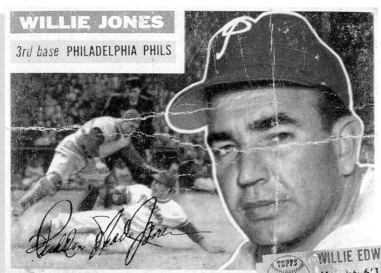

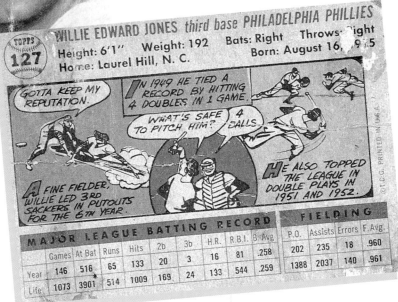

Some veteran collectors remember the days when a baseball card, such as this 1956 Topps card of Philadelphia Phillies third baseman Willie "Puddin' Head" Jones, featured single- or multi-panel cartoons on the back recounting highlights from the player's career.

Prior to visiting a shop, sit down and determine the individual cards or card sets you'd like to obtain (note the card company, year, player names, card numbers, and so on) and their values as listed in the latest price guides. Jot down your facts on a piece of paper to take with you. That way, if you get nervous or flustered and forget what you intended to ask the dealer, you'll still have the written information at your fingertips.

Once inside the shop, browse around. That way you'll get a feel for what the owner carries and the prices you can expect to pay; plus, something that you hadn't previously thought about collecting may catch your eye.

Cards are displayed in a variety of ways, including vinyl sheets and rigid plastic holders. All collectors—beginners and experts alike—should ask the dealer to see the card out of its vinyl covering or plastic holder, because these storage devices can hide scratches, creases, notches, and stains that otherwise are difficult to detect. It's the best way to ensure that the item you are thinking about buying is priced according to its actual condition.

Buying factory-sealed sets is another matter. If you discover later that a card is missing, or that several cards have severe creases or some other manufacturing defect in them, you cannot hold the retailer responsible. He or she is under no obligation to replace the offending cards, although a few dealers will do just that as a courtesy to their customers. If you buy a set that the dealer has hand-collated from wax packs or another configuration and there are problems, then the dealer *is* responsible for keeping the customer satisfied.

If you've spotted a nice-looking card that you'd like to own, say, one from the 1960s priced at $20, it's perfectly OK to wheel and deal with the retailer. But don't insult the person by making a pointless offer to pay $10 for the item. If the amount is a little more than what you can afford to pay, simply ask the dealer if he or she would be willing to come down on the price of that card. Never badger a dealer or whine about a refusal to lower the price on an item you want. That kind of behavior will nix a deal in a heartbeat.

You have other avenues through which to buy your cards, including hobby shows and conventions, auctions, and mail-order dealers.

Shopping by mail has become increasingly popular among card collectors for several reasons: convenience, variety, and the occasional discounts on large purchases. But there are some simple guidelines to follow when shopping by mail:

First, read the fine print. This seems so basic, yet collectors sometimes fail to catch statements such as "prices subject to change without notice." Dealers don't put this in their ads to take advantage of unsuspecting collectors;

1941
World War II affects the baseball card industry, much as World War I did, but not before Gum issues its only color set.

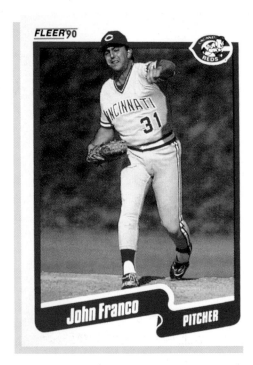

John Franco's 1990 Fleer card, which was issued as part of that firm's major set early in 1990, is an example of a card "before its time": Franco was traded in the 1989–90 off-season, and played the 1990 season in a Mets uniform. That's why updated/traded sets, which appear later in the season, are so popular with hobbyists.

they do it because they must submit their ad copy to a publication at least a month or more in advance of when the publication hits the newsstands. The market value of an item can change dramatically, slightly, or not at all during that period. So, always call the mail-order dealer first, to get the latest price quote on the items you want.

Second, if the dealer offers the option, charge your order. While paying with a credit card typically costs more, because of the surcharge covering the credit card company's fees, it can also act as a safety net for the collector who either changes his mind and decides to cancel his order or is for any reason unhappy with his order, because he can then refuse to pay that particular charge on his bill and the credit card company may help to resolve the matter.

Third, determine your shipping costs. Some dealers charge a flat fee to cover shipping, while others base their shipping charges on the dollar amount of the purchase. A few dealers will absorb the shipping charges themselves if they feel the order is a substantial one.

Finally, when you place your order, write down the name of the person who took your order, as well as the estimated date of delivery. Some order-takers will automatically repeat your name (and its spelling), your address, the items ordered, and your credit card number before hanging up the telephone. Make sure yours does. You don't want your order to wind up on the doorstep of someone whose street address is just one digit different from your own.

If you haven't received your order by the date promised, contact the dealer to see what's up. Don't assume the worst. Legitimate delays can result when an item is temporarily out of stock. Be firm, but be polite. If you're still unhappy with the service, ask for a refund.

Sadly, some delays are caused by ripoff artists who never intended to send you the goods in the first place. If that's the case contact the publication that ran the ad. Its publisher and editorial staff can make it very unpleasant

BILL GOODWIN'S TIPS FOR MAIL-ORDER CUSTOMERS

A full-time dealer since 1986, St. Louisan Bill Goodwin specializes in quality, older baseball cards, and sports memorabilia. He's a regular at hobby shows around the country. But his mail-order business, St. Louis Baseball Cards, which he operates with his wife and children, is his bread and butter. A devotee of 1950s and 1960s cards, Goodwin offers several tips on ordering by mail:

1. Phone and reserve the cards you want, especially if they're older cards, because of their desirability with collectors.

2. Typically, a dealer will hold a card for seven working days, though some will extend the deadline; if it's going to take you longer to send your check or money order, be sure to let the dealer know.

3. Include with your money order or check some sort of letter or note that clearly states what you are ordering.

4. Make sure your return address is legible.

5. Make sure your return address is current; Bill tells of the time when a customer moved without informing anyone, and UPS was unable to deliver a $3,900 order.

6. Never reserve a card you're not sure you are going to buy. Nothing is more frustrating for a dealer than to hold a card for someone and receive three other inquiries on it while the original caller wavers on the purchase; dealers hate to lose business that way.

7. Don't skimp on the shipping charges. Some people want their purchases sent to them in envelopes, which is a good way to invite trouble—evidenced by the customer who provided Goodwin with a self-addressed, stamped envelope, which someone opened easily to remove the valuable card.

for a dealer that fails to deliver, even to the extent of suspending that dealer's advertising privileges. Fortunately for you and for the hobby as a whole, "worst-case scenarios" like this are rare. Reputable dealers don't like the ripoff artist any more than you do, because it hurts the hobby that they've helped to build.

SELLING YOUR CARDS TO A DEALER

Some dealers are more exacting than others when they grade older cards for retail. So it's a good idea to shop around and compare prices and quality before plunking down your hard-earned cash for an item that you may later find in the same condition at a lower price. Using that same reasoning, it's also a good idea to visit several card shops before attempting to sell your cards.

It's not uncommon for dealers to follow what's known as the half-price rule during the grading process. If a particular card you wish to sell is deemed by the dealer to be in perfect condition (sharp corners, even borders, no wax stains), the dealer should assign the card's retail value toward the high end of its listing in one of the current price guides.

But if one of the corners is bent or an edge is beginning to fray, the price is automatically dropped by half of its book value. For example, if ''Joe Player's'' rookie card in mint condition is listed in the price guides at $30, its value drops to $15 if just one corner is slightly bent or if there is a crease in it somewhere. And, in the dealer's eyes, another serious defect will probably drop the retail value of that card to $7.50, and so on.

Most dealers will only offer you from 50 to 70 percent of your card's retail (book) value, anyway, though a few dealers may offer to pay you an amount slightly above or below those ''limits.'' (In older cards, particularly ones that are rare and/or feature big name players, dealers frequently are more lenient when it comes to wear and tear.)

Getting back to the example of Joe Player's rookie card: If the dealer plans to sell that $15 card at a profit, he or she may offer you something in the neighborhood of $10 for it.

So, know what you have and grade your cards accordingly; expect to get less than book value regardless of who's on the card; and know the lowest price you will

<hr>

1948
Bowman (formerly Gum), then Leaf, issue card sets; Leaf exits market after issuing 1949 set, half of which is now very rare.

No. 34 of a Series of 240

DAVE KOSLO

Pitcher—New York Giants

Born: Menasha, Wisc., March 31, 1920
Bats: Left Throws: Left Ht.: 5:11 Wt.: 180
He became a big leaguer at end of 1941 season.
After compiling a 13-13 record with Milwaukee
in American Association he appeared in 4 games
for Giants, winning 1 and losing 2. Divided next
season between New York and Jersey City.
Then came 3 years in military service. When
he returned to Giants he became a starting
pitcher. His 1946 record was 14-19; 1947 was
15-10 and last season he won 8 and lost 10.

#202—OFFICIAL BASEBALL RING
Made of durable metal. Adjustable—fits any size finger.
Beautiful silverplate oxidized finish brings out detail of
official Baseball Emblem. Baseball of
white plastic. Sides of ring show Baseball
and Crossed Bats design. Send only
15c and 3 Baseball wrappers to:
BASEBALL, P.O. BOX 491
NEW YORK 46, N.Y.

(Not valid where contrary to State laws)
Offer expires 12/31/49 ©Bowman Gum, Inc., 1949

accept for your cards.

Keep in mind, too, that because of fan loyalties, cards
of one team or a particular player are not going to bring
the same dollar amounts in every region of the country.
A pristine card of Will Clark will not garner the
same excitement in New York City that it would in
San Francisco. Know your market.

Special mail-in offers advertised on card backs have long been a part of the hobby. This Dave Koslo card from the 1949 Bowman set touts a ring, while in the same set another card might entice collectors with a game and coin bank.

OTHER MEANS OF SELLING YOUR CARDS

While for many collectors the preferred method for selling
one's cards is the local card shop, especially if those cards
are current issues, there are other avenues at your dis-
posal. Another common means of selling off your cards is
through classified ads in your local newspaper or in

nationally distributed hobby publications.

Naturally, classified ads vary in price, so do your home-work and find out how much it will cost you to run your ad and how many readers (and potential buyers) it will reach. You have to weigh the cost of such advertising with what you realistically expect to get in return from the cards you sell.

For beginning collectors, especially, it's best not to attempt to sell off any current cards via printed ads, because established dealers offer very competitive prices on them.

There may be private collectors in your area who would consider buying your cards from you, though they would more likely be interested in older, harder-to-find issues than cards of today's players. Private collectors generally are quite knowledgeable about the hobby and about the value of certain cards. Like any other group of serious collectors, they can drive a hard bargain, so be ready to negotiate.

TRADING: IT ISN'T DEAD, IT JUST LOOKS FUNNY

It isn't necessary to fork over your loose change every time you see a wax pack or cello pack or rack pack to get what you need.

When it comes to filling out your own card collection, don't forget about that long lost art of trading with other local enthusiasts. Maybe the kid down the block or some fellow students at your school or someone who plays in the same organized baseball program as you do would be interested in swapping.

While it can be difficult to find collectors—even younger ones—who are not obsessed with values, card trading between collectors is as old as the hobby itself and offers a lot of fun.

> **1951**
> Topps enters baseball card market with two sets—known as the Blue Backs and Red Backs —each consisting of 52 cards.

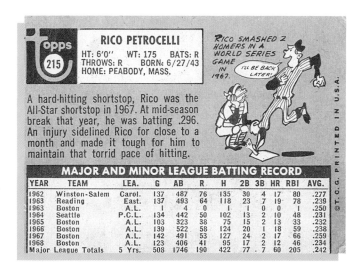

RICO PETROCELLI
Topps 215
HT: 6'0" WT: 175 BATS: R
THROWS: R BORN: 6/27/43
HOME: PEABODY, MASS.

RICO SMASHED 2 HOMERS IN A WORLD SERIES GAME IN 1967. "I'LL BE BACK LATER!"

© T.C.G. PRINTED IN U.S.A.

A hard-hitting shortstop, Rico was the All-Star shortstop in 1967. At mid-season break that year, he was batting .296. An injury sidelined Rico for close to a month and made it tough for him to maintain that torrid pace of hitting.

MAJOR AND MINOR LEAGUE BATTING RECORD

YEAR	TEAM	LEA.	G	AB	R	H	2B	3B	HR	RBI	AVG.
1962	Winston-Salem	Carol.	137	487	76	135	30	4	17	80	.277
1963	Reading	East.	137	493	64	118	23	7	19	78	.239
1963	Boston	A.L.	1	4	0	1	1	0	0	1	.250
1964	Seattle	P.C.L.	134	442	50	102	13	2	10	48	.231
1965	Boston	A.L.	103	323	38	75	15	2	13	33	.232
1966	Boston	A.L.	139	522	58	124	20	1	18	59	.238
1967	Boston	A.L.	142	491	53	127	24	2	17	66	.259
1968	Boston	A.L.	123	406	41	95	17	2	12	46	.234
Major League Totals	5 Yrs.		508	1746	190	422	77	7	60	205	.242

In near-mint condition, Rico Petrocelli's 1969 Topps card (here) can be had for less than a buck. His 1970 Topps card, however, which shows his ''career year'' stats of 1969, goes for nearly three times as much in near-mint condition.

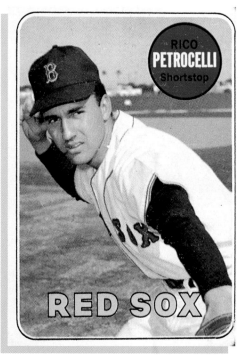

When trading cards, the best thing to do is to appraise your cards fairly and accurately according to grading standards set forth in the latest price guides. Likewise, be fair and accurate when judging someone else's cards. Trading can be time-consuming, so patience is a virtue.

As for trading with dealers, there are rules to follow and things to know.

Dealers rarely, if ever, trade for equal value. That's because there is overhead for shop owners and setup costs for convention dealers. Because a dealer is getting an item, rather than money, for the item you covet, he or she must offset that lack of money by getting additional items for resale at some future date.

Generally speaking, dealers offer a two-for-one trade, which means that if you desire a $15 card in the dealer's display case, you will probably have to trade at least $30 worth of cards before the dealer will even begin to consider the swap.

Of course, your willingness to trade away $30 or more worth of cards is no guarantee the dealer will go for it, because the dealer must be completely confident that what he or she is getting from you can be sold to another collector—for *cash*—within a reasonable amount of time.

Some dealers will forsake the two-for-one trade if you have something they are most anxious to acquire, either for another customer, or to add to their own collection.

Occasionally, trades involve different objects—for instance, an autographed ball from a Hall of Famer for a vintage World Series press pin. As long as each collector is receiving something of quality, something that each wants, the relative "value" of either item becomes meaningless. Trading, while less a factor in the hobby than it once was, can still be an interesting, satisfying way of obtaining that special card or other collectible.

VALUABLE CARDS AND CARD SETS

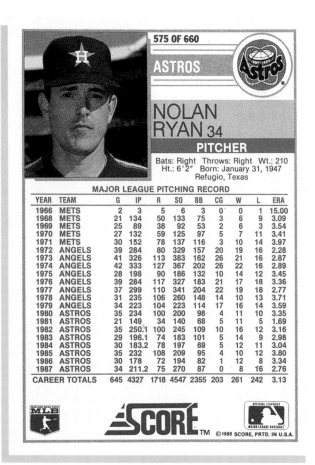

ASTROS

NOLAN RYAN 34

PITCHER

Bats: Right   Throws: Right   Wt.: 210
Ht.: 6'2"   Born: January 31, 1947
Refugio, Texas

MAJOR LEAGUE PITCHING RECORD										
YEAR	TEAM	G	IP	R	SO	BB	CG	W	L	ERA
1966	METS	2	3	5	6	3	0	0	1	15.00
1968	METS	21	134	50	133	75	3	6	9	3.09
1969	METS	25	89	38	92	53	2	6	3	3.54
1970	METS	27	132	59	125	97	5	7	11	3.41
1971	METS	30	152	78	137	116	3	10	14	3.97
1972	ANGELS	39	284	80	329	157	20	19	16	2.28
1973	ANGELS	41	326	113	383	162	26	21	16	2.87
1974	ANGELS	42	333	127	367	202	26	22	16	2.89
1975	ANGELS	28	198	90	186	132	10	14	12	3.45
1976	ANGELS	39	284	117	327	183	21	17	18	3.36
1977	ANGELS	37	299	110	341	204	22	19	18	2.77
1978	ANGELS	31	235	106	260	148	14	10	13	3.71
1979	ANGELS	34	223	104	223	114	17	16	14	3.59
1980	ASTROS	35	234	100	200	98	4	11	10	3.35
1981	ASTROS	21	149	34	140	68	5	11	5	1.69
1982	ASTROS	35	250.1	100	245	109	10	16	12	3.16
1983	ASTROS	29	196.1	74	183	101	5	14	9	2.98
1984	ASTROS	30	183.2	78	197	69	5	12	11	3.04
1985	ASTROS	35	232	108	209	95	4	10	12	3.80
1986	ASTROS	30	178	72	194	82	1	12	8	3.34
1987	ASTROS	34	211.2	75	270	87	0	8	16	2.76
CAREER TOTALS		645	4327	1718	4547	2355	203	261	242	3.13

SCORE™   © 1988 SCORE, PRTD. IN U.S.A.

Only the strong survive: It's a good thing Score chose not to include Nolan Ryan's minor league stats on the back of his 1988 card—there's no room. (Incidentally, minor league stats are useful for filling the cards of those players who haven't seen a lot of big-league time.)

That baseball card you're holding in your hand…how much do you think it's worth? If you're like most beginning collectors, putting a price tag on it does not come easily. After all, the card may depict your favorite player or team. It may have been difficult for you to obtain. You may have paid a considerable amount of money for it. It may be the card that completes a set you've spent years assembling.

Any or all of these things will make that card seem—to you, anyway—priceless. Part with that card? Not on your life, you answer. But while collecting baseball cards or other memorabilia has always been a somewhat personal quest, there are two basic factors in this hobby that determine *any* card's value: condition and subject.

A card's physical condition usually carries the most

Score debuted in 1988 as the fifth major firm of nationally distributed baseball cards. The cards were noted for their sharp, full-color photos on front and back, and made a big impression on collectors.

NOLAN RYAN
P

weight with collectors. Regardless of who or what is on the card—one of today's superstars or a team photo of an "also ran" from decades ago—if it's in tip-top condition it will be worth more than the same card in so-so condition. But even a scarce card in average shape can come with a hefty price tag if there is a demand for it. And "commons"—cards picturing players of average talent—will sometimes have greater value than cards of today's superstars *if* they are uncommonly rare.

And, as you might expect, older cards picturing Hall of Famers and other big names of the past tend to be among the most prized collectibles in the hobby, especially if they are in mint or near-mint condition. To understand how dealers and collectors classify cards according to condition, let's take a look at the definitions of mint, near-mint,

The tremendous popularity of baseball card collecting encompasses minor league cards, too. Many hobbyists enjoy putting together complete sets of their favorite farm teams, teams which may include a future big league star or two in the making.

and other grading terms.

Keep in mind when you read the following explanations that while these classifications are generally accepted within the hobby world, two perfectly competent and honorable hobbyists may not agree on the condition of a given card. Grading, like collecting itself, contains the human element known as difference of opinion.

MINT (M or MT) A card that is in perfect condition; which means that the corners are sharp, the picture is perfectly focused and centered (meaning that the borders are even all the way around), that no smudges, creases, or other defects are present, and that the card's colors are bright and in perfect register.

NEAR-MINT (NrMT) A card with a barely discernable defect, including but not limited to any one of the following: layering; slight loss in color brightness or overall surface gloss; borders slightly off-center; slightly rounded corners; some wear on the edges.

EXCELLENT-MINT (EX-MT) A card with two or three of the above slight defects.

EXCELLENT (EX or E) A card containing a few minor flaws, such as slightly rounded corners, a border that's not the same as the others, minor wear on edges, color just barely faded, slight loss in surface gloss.

VERY GOOD (VG) A card that has been handled but not mistreated; it will show somewhat uneven borders, minor discoloration, notching, layering, or scuffing; the photo itself may be slightly out of focus.

GOOD (G) A card past its prime, with noticeable wear on its edges or corners, some color fading or loss of surface sheen, uneven borders, layering, notching, and other easily seen defects.

FAIR (F) A card with substantial notching, creases, badly uneven or missing borders, substantial discoloration and/or layering, damaged edges, and so on.

POOR (P) A card whose best days are only a memory—meaning, its only value may be to collectors attempting to complete a set until a card of better quality comes along. These cards are in poor condition, with badly frayed corners and edges, horrible color or little color at all, extreme creasing or notching, and even writing on them.

> ### 1952
> Topps issues its first major set (407 cards in full color), including the most popular Mickey Mantle card which today is valued at about $8,000.

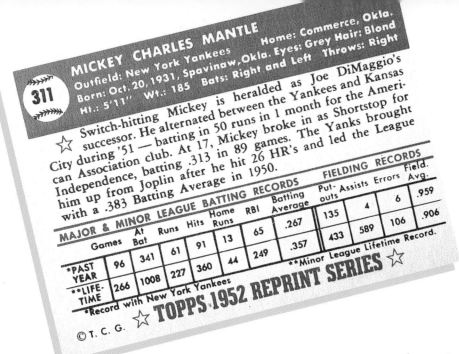

MICKEY CHARLES MANTLE
Outfield: New York Yankees   Home: Commerce, Okla.
Born: Oct. 20, 1931, Spavinaw, Okla. Eyes: Grey Hair: Blond
Ht.: 5'11"   Wt.: 185 Bats: Right and Left Throws: Right

☆ Switch-hitting Mickey is heralded as Joe DiMaggio's successor. He alternated between the Yankees and Kansas City during '51 — batting in 50 runs in 1 month for the American Association club. At 17, Mickey broke in as Shortstop for Independence, batting .313 in 89 games. The Yanks brought him up from Joplin after he hit 26 HR's and led the League with a .383 Batting Average in 1950.

| MAJOR & MINOR LEAGUE BATTING RECORDS | | | | | | | FIELDING RECORDS | | | |
	Games	At Bat	Runs	Hits	Home Runs	RBI	Batting Average	Put-outs	Assists	Errors	Field. Avg.
*PAST YEAR	96	341	61	91	13	65	.267	135	4	6	.959
**LIFE-TIME	266	1008	227	360	44	249	.357	433	589	106	.906

*Record with New York Yankees   **Minor League Lifetime Record.

☆ TOPPS 1952 REPRINT SERIES ☆

© T. C. G.

If a set is a reprint, the manufacturer should say so somewhere on the cards to avoid confusion and possible misunderstanding between buyer and seller. While reprint cards have little intrinsic value, they serve a useful purpose: They enable collectors to own classic issues of the past for very little money.

1953
Bowman issues the first set of its kind: actual color photos are reproduced on the cards, and they become instant classics.

In addition to these classifications, the hobby will occasionally use in-between grades such as ''fair-to-good'' (F-G) or ''very good-to-excellent'' (VG-E) to define the condition of a card or card set.

To further confuse the issue, not all grading systems are worded exactly alike, as you will soon find when reading various hobby publications and price guides on the subject of baseball cards. There are subtle differences, to be sure, but they may come into play when buying cards from a variety of dealers. It wouldn't hurt to ask the individual dealers what grading system they use to price their cards.

Sometimes, a card's condition will take a back seat to its subject. For instance, many of the early-twentieth-century tobacco cards that are still in circulation are far from being classified as mint or near-mint by today's

The original 1952 Topps Mickey Mantle card in top condition is one of the more popular—and expensive—collectibles in the hobby. Most collectors can't afford paying thousands of dollars for an original, but they can afford a reproduction of it, like this one.

tough standards, yet collectors pay premium prices for them. Why? Because they are scarce or, in hobby lingo, rare.

Likewise, the Mickey Mantle card (#311) from the 1952 Topps set is one of the hobby's most cherished mementos. Even in less than mint condition it commands respect (and thousands of dollars). "The Mick" is a Hall-of-Famer, of course, and one of the most popular players to grace a Major League uniform. But his card is also valuable because it is rare. And when a card is rare and the demand for it is high, most serious collectors won't even blink when the conversation finally turns to money.

Not all rare cards are in great demand, however, regardless of their condition or the players pictured. The best places to learn more about what's hot and what's not are the hobby publications, your local card shop, and hobby shows. Keeping informed will enable you to make wise decisions in your buying and selling habits and may help you to get in on the ground floor when a "sleeper" card suddenly wakes up to a newfound popularity among collectors, sending its value skyward.

So, know and understand how a card is graded, find out the number of copies of the card that are "out there," and learn about the player (or players) featured on that card. Both from the standpoint of collecting for the fun of it and collecting for investment purposes, the more you read and talk and learn about baseball cards, the more enjoyment you'll get from the hobby. Information will remain your greatest tool as you work your way from beginning collector to expert.

HOBBY SHOWS, CONVENTIONS, AND THE NATIONAL

Topps entered the scene in 1951 with a variety of unique card sets, including one titled ''Connie Mack's All-Stars'' that spotlighted 11 Hall of Famers. The die-cut cards featured a foldable background that enabled the card to stand up. Today, those cards which have been left unfolded are worth much more than those that have been folded (some say mutilated). ''The Bambino'' was on card #9 in the 11-card set of ''Connie Mack's All-Stars'' issued by Topps in 1951. In near-mint condition, it is the most valuable card in the set (more than $1,500). The firm also released a similar 11-card set of contemporary All-Stars that year that included Larry Doby, Ralph Kiner, and Yogi Berra.

GEORGE HERMAN RUTH
1894   OUTFIELD   1948

Babe Ruth

**CONNIE MACK'S
ALL-TIME ALL-STAR TEAM**

*L*ike a kid in a candy store. That's how many collectors, young and old, feel when they attend a major hobby show or convention.

In all directions they see tables full of baseball cards of every era, autographed photos, bats and baseballs, pennants from seasons past, vintage World Series programs, bobbing-head dolls, Hartland statues, big league uniforms and warm-up jackets, used tabletop games, sports video cassettes, posters of superstar athletes, baseball caps, out-of-print books and magazines, and many other eye-catching collectibles.

People attend these gatherings for various reasons. Some are looking for specific items that will complete their collections. Others hope to find a bargain on the latest major card sets. A few simply want to browse or to

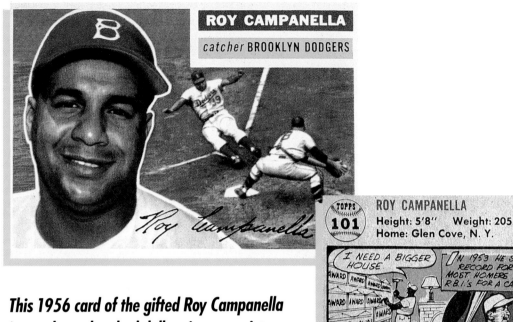

ROY CAMPANELLA
catcher BROOKLYN DODGERS

TOPPS
101

ROY CAMPANELLA | *catcher* BROOKLYN DODGERS
Height: 5'8"   Weight: 205   Bats: Right   Throws: Right
Home: Glen Cove, N. Y.   Born: November 19, 1921

I NEED A BIGGER HOUSE.

IN 1953 HE SET A RECORD FOR THE MOST HOMERS AND R.B.I.'s FOR A CATCHER

WHO PUT THAT WALL HERE?

ROY WAS VOTED NATIONAL LEAGUE MOST VALUABLE PLAYER IN '55 FOR THE 3RD TIME.

A GREAT DEFENSIVE STAR, ROY LED THE N.L. BACKSTOPS IN PUTOUTS 5 TIMES.

| MAJOR LEAGUE BATTING RECORD | | | | | | | | | FIELDING | | | |
	Games	At Bat	Runs	Hits	2b	3b	H.R.	R.B.I	B.Avg	P.O.	Assists	Errors	F.Avg.
Year	123	446	81	142	20	1	32	107	.318	672	54	6	.992
Life	988	3487	557	996	163	17	209	721	.286	5243	450	69	.988

This 1956 card of the gifted Roy Campanella is worth one hundred dollars in near-mint condition, but his worth to the Brooklyn Dodgers was immeasurable during their glory years in the 1950s. The line stats shown here are for the 1955 season, the third and last time ''Campy'' won the National League's Most Valuable Player award.

talk with their fellow hobbyists. And a growing number of collectors are there to get the signatures of famous baseball players and other athletes—retired or current—who are on hand for the event.

Whatever your reason for going, you're taking part in one of the hobby's more prominent activities. On any given weekend, dozens of smaller shows and several larger conventions are in full swing all across the United States. Their importance to the hobby has increased dramatically since the early 1980s, when collecting baseball cards and related memorabilia really took off with the American public.

Not only do they provide a bustling marketplace for dealers and collectors wanting to buy, sell, and trade their items, but these events also help maintain interest in a

hobby that just a few years ago was little more than a casual undertaking by a relatively small group of die-hards. These days, entire families are into collecting.

Smaller shows typically involve from a dozen to fifty or sixty dealer tables, while the larger gatherings feature as many as one hundred dealers. Major conventions boast several hundred dealer tables. Shows normally run one or two days, while the National Sports Collectors Convention, held each July in a different U.S. city, runs for the better part of a three-day weekend.

Most, but not all, shows charge an admission fee. Expect to pay a buck or two for the smaller shows, and up to $5 or more for the big events. Also, expect to pay a fee to obtain the autographs of special guests.

Print ads announcing the show usually provide the details on autograph signings ahead of time, but check with the folks at the admission table to verify the fees and guidelines. (Some guests charge more for signing balls and bats; others refuse to sign anything other than flat items, that is, cards and pictures.) Don't be surprised by some of the signing fees, either. It is not uncommon to pay ten times the admission fee to get a single item autographed by a baseball Hall of Famer or other superstar athlete.

Keep in mind that you have a limited amount of money to spend at one of these shows. Know what you want before you drive to the show site. Get there early if you expect a huge crowd. Don't be swayed by the very first table you see, especially for newer items that are in large supply. Shop around. Remember, these hobby dealers are competing with one another for your dollar, so it's wise to avoid impulse buying.

Take a notepad and pen or pencil, and jot down prices as you move from table to table. That way, you'll have a record of which dealers are offering the best buys on the items you want. If the prices are not plainly marked, simply ask the dealers what they're charging. You may wish to inquire about discounts on quantity purchases, too.

1955
Bowman's last hurrah is a 320-card effort that includes 31 umpire cards, an industry first; card borders are "TV sets".

TOM OWENS'S TIPS FOR AUTOGRAPH HOUNDS

*A*t one point in the film *The Natural,* baseball star Roy Hobbs (played by Robert Redford) is shown signing autographs for adoring youngsters.

Despite the popularity of hobby shows and conventions that spotlight big-name athletes of the past and present who (for a fee) sign baseball cards, photos, and other items, many fans still wade into the middle of a crowd or hang over the railing, waving a scorecard in the person's face and pleading for an autograph.

Here are some common-sense tips from veteran autograph collector Tom Owens, author of *Collecting Sports Autographs,* to help you increase your chances of success:

1. Treat the ballplayer as a human being; be polite, and use "please" and "thank you" during the exchange.

2. Be reasonable—don't ask the ballplayer to sign five of the same card or photo; many athletes today are paranoid that the autograph seeker is going to get rich from selling their (free) autographs.

3. The best time to get the player's signature is *before* a crowd has developed.

4. Don't be afraid to speak to the ballplayer if you have the time; if you've seen him play, tell him so, and wish him good luck in his future; this polite but warmhearted approach often elicits a better response from the player than to simply ask for his signature and then cease talking.

5. Have in your hand the item you want to have signed; don't make the person stand and wait while you rummage through your jacket or purse looking for it.

6. Use *only* a ballpoint pen for signing baseballs; Sharpie permanent markers (made by Sanford) are preferred for cards, photos, and bats but *not* for baseballs, because the ink will eventually bleed into the baseball's hide.

7. Have the pen or Sharpie uncapped as you hand it to the person, and always carry extras, just in case.

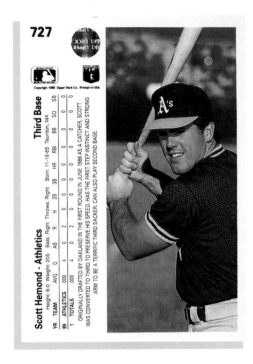

Scott Hemond struck this pose for his baseball card, but he never got the chance to swing the bat in a big league game in his debut season of 1989. His four appearances with the eventual World Champions were all as a pinch runner. At least he scored twice.

Finally, don't let a dealer pressure you with a corny, hard-sell line such as "I can't promise you that it'll be here when you come back" or "These are among my biggest sellers, and you won't find a better deal on 'em anywhere else."

By keeping these simple guidelines in mind, you'll increase your enjoyment of any show or convention you attend, while decreasing your chances for disappointment. Card shows and conventions are the number one place to pick up the items you want at competitive prices. Best of all, they are great fun.

"THE NATIONAL"

Major League Baseball has its annual All-Star Game. And every year for more than a decade, baseball card collectors have had their National Sports Collectors Convention. Each is a mid-season showcase for its participants and sponsors. So, if the All-Star Game brings together the best and most talented ballplayers, then "the National" brings together the best dealers and most avid collectors from around the world.

"The atmosphere at the National is unmistakable... exciting...colorful," says Bill Goodwin, of St. Louis Baseball Cards. "It's the one time of the year when virtually everyone in the hobby has an opportunity to gather in one place. People—and not just the dealers, either—are coming in from all over the country, and families are making vacations out of it.

"While the dealers hope to make money, obviously, the atmosphere at the National is more one of kinship, camaraderie. We have the softball and basketball contests, the card-flipping contest, the APBA or Stratomatic tabletop games, and things of that nature. It's a time for old friends to see one another and for new friendships to be formed. I hope the hobby always has the National. It's an enjoyable time for everybody."

Echoing Goodwin's sentiments is Wanda Marcus, the

TOM OWENS'S TIPS FOR AUTOGRAPHS BY MAIL

1. If he's a current player, write to him in care of his home ballpark, never to his residence.
2. If he's retired, write to him at his home (*The Sport Americana Baseball Address List,* an inexpensive paperback updated every two years, will help you with this).
3. Never send a form letter.
4. Always include a self-addressed, stamped envelope with your request; don't expect the player to pay postage on the item you're asking him to sign and send back to you.

Owens also notes this important consideration:

"Some non-autograph collectors are unimpressed by signed baseball cards. They view a mint card that's autographed to be simply defaced, and will have no interest in even paying price guide value for the card, let alone more value. Some purists don't care about autographed cards; so collectors who are thinking about selling their cards at some future date— but who still enjoy autograph collecting—might want to get those signatures on photos or index cards in order to keep their baseball cards in their original condition."

Arlington, Texas–based dealer who, along with her husband, John, has twice hosted the National, once in 1986 and again in 1990. She has collected cards and other baseball memorabilia for more than twenty-five years. In the mid-1970s, she became a dealer, and in 1982 promoted her first hobby show. "I think you could have a 2500-table show if you gave everybody a table who requested one," Marcus says of the staggering increase in the number of dealers and collectors attending the National since the first one was held in 1980 in Los Angeles.

"The National is important to the hobby because you get all the elite of the hobby in one convention center over one single weekend of the year," Marcus adds. "It runs the gamut, too, from dealers who frequently set up at the smaller weekend shows around the country to dealers who normally run their own shops each weekend and the only show they attend in any given year *is* the National.

"One of the best things about the National is the tremendous variety of collectibles the dealers offer. Not only are there more items from which to choose, but some dealers save their best merchandise to display at the National. You might see a Babe Ruth or a Lou Gehrig jersey at one table, or a Jackie Robinson collectible.

"Some of the things are not for sale, but the dealers display them anyway, both to draw attention to their tables and to allow fans to view a piece of baseball history that they might not otherwise get to see," says Marcus.

According to Marcus, when she and her husband hosted the National in 1986, some 20,000 people were in attendance for the three-day event. Four years later, attendance had nearly *doubled*. Also, the current or former sports figures who are guest signers at the National (and at regional shows and conventions, to some extent) represent not only baseball but other major sports, too, including football, hockey, basketball, and boxing.

To learn the dates and location for upcoming National Sports Collectors Conventions, check with your local dealer, and read the major hobby publications.

OTHER COLLECTIBLES

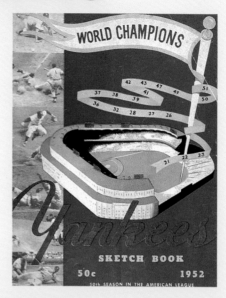

Baseball cards remain the hobby's No. 1 collectible, but there is a wealth of other neat stuff to consider. Like cards, sketch books, such as this one recalling the New York Yankees' exciting 1951 season, serve as fascinating records of bygone eras.

Baseball cards remain the number one baseball collectible for the nation's hobbyists, but there are many other kinds of memorabilia that are fun to collect and enjoy, too.

And, as with baseball cards, you can spend a little or a lot; acquire a one-of-a-kind item or several similar items to form your own unique set; display your treasures or store them for safekeeping until you decide to sell them.

The best place to go for ideas is a weekend hobby show, especially if it features a sizable number of dealers from your region or possibly from around the country. There for sale, among the thousands and thousands of baseball cards, is a fascinating array of autographed balls, bats, and photos; press pins, pennants, and buttons; caps, uniforms, and plaques; toy figurines and tabletop games;

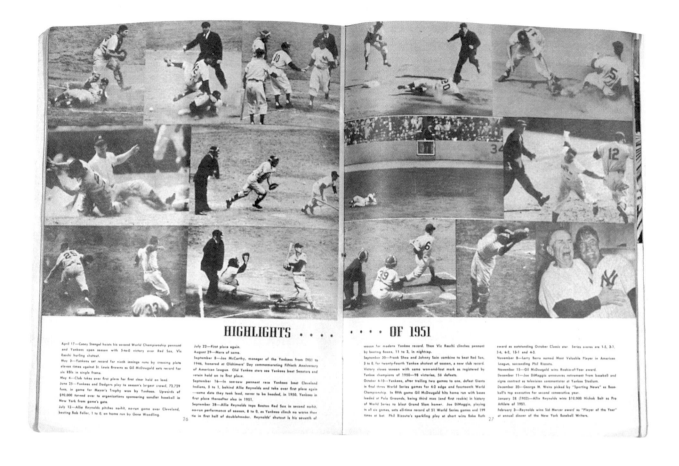

HIGHLIGHTS . . . . OF 1951

April 17—Casey Stengel hoists his second World Championship pennant and Yankees open season with 5-to-0 victory over Red Sox, Vic Raschi hurling shutout.

May 3—Yankees set record for ninth innings runs by crossing plate eleven times against St. Louis Browns as Gil McDougald sets record for six RBIs in single frame.

May 4—Club takes over first place for first clear hold on lead.

June 25—Yankees and Dodgers play to season's largest crowd, 73,729 fans, in game for Mayor's Trophy won by Yankees. Upwards of $90,000 turned over to organizations sponsoring sandlot baseball in New York from game's gate.

July 12—Allie Reynolds pitches no-hit, no-run game over Cleveland, beating Bob Feller, 1 to 0, on home run by Gene Woodling.

July 22—First place again.

August 29—More of same.

September 8—Joe McCarthy, manager of the Yankees from 1931 to 1946, honored at Oldtimers' Day commemorating Fiftieth Anniversary of American League. Old Yankee stars see Yankees beat Senators and retain hold on to first place.

September 16—In see-saw pennant race Yankees beat Cleveland Indians, 5 to 1, behind Allie Reynolds and take over first place again—same date they took lead, never to be headed, in 1950. Yankees in first place thereafter also in 1951.

September 28—Allie Reynolds tops Boston Red Sox in second no-hit, no-run performance of season, 8 to 0, as Yankees clinch no worse than tie in first half of doubleheader. Reynolds' shutout is his seventh of

season for modern Yankee record. Then Vic Raschi clinches pennant by beating Boston, 11 to 3, in nightcap.

September 30—Frank Shea and Johnny Sain combine to beat Red Sox, 3 to 0, for twenty-fourth Yankee shutout of season, a new club record. Victory closes season with same won-and-lost mark as registered by Yankee champions of 1950—98 victories, 56 defeats.

October 4-10—Yankees, after trailing two games to one, defeat Giants in final three World Series games for 4-2 edge and fourteenth World Championship. In fifth game Gil McDougald hits home run with bases loaded at Polo Grounds, being third man (and first rookie) in history of World Series to blast Grand Slam homer. Joe DiMaggio, playing in all six games, sets all-time record of 51 World Series games and 199 times at bat. Phil Rizzuto's sparkling play at short wins Babe Ruth

award as outstanding October Classic star. Series scores are 1-5, 3-1, 2-6, 6-2, 13-1 and 4-3.

November 8—Larry Berra named Most Valuable Player in American League, succeeding Phil Rizzuto.

November 15—Gil McDougald wins Rookie-of-Year award.

December 11—Joe DiMaggio announces retirement from baseball and signs contract as television commentator at Yankee Stadium.

December 20—George M. Weiss picked by "Sporting News" as Baseball's top executive for second consecutive year.

January 28 (1952)—Allie Reynolds wins $10,000 Hickok Belt as Pro Athlete of 1951.

February 5—Reynolds wins Sid Mercer award as "Player of the Year" at annual dinner of the New York Baseball Writers.

26   27

World Series and All-Star Game programs; and suitable-for-framing prints of your favorite athletes.

And that's just the beginning. At larger hobby shows and, of course, the National Sports Collectors Convention held each July in a different major city, you'll find such a huge selection of baseball collectibles that it can be nearly as overwhelming as all the cards on display.

But remember: it's a hobby that's meant to be fun, and you should collect what you like without getting too concerned about what an item will be worth somewhere down the line. As with any investment you make, the value of noncard collectibles will rise and fall in the hobby marketplace. Your main thought when considering purchasing any piece of baseball memorabilia should be "Will this be something that I will enjoy having—does it have

special meaning for me or for someone in my family?"

Another consideration should be whether you want to own just one of something or want to build an entire collection of related items. For instance, would owning a game-used bat from a Hall of Fame player such as Cubs' great Billy Williams appeal to you, or would owning game-used bats of several Hall of Famers be a goal worth pursuing?

Or, how about this: You were born in 1961, the year the legendary Maris-and-Mantle-led New York Yankees were crowned World Champions. You could acquire a World Series program for the 1961 Yankees-Reds Fall Classic and display it proudly among your other memorabilia, or you might want to use it as the starting point for a larger collection of World Series programs. How about every Series involving the Yankees? Every Series played in the decade of the 1960s? Every Series since your birth year? See how this works? There is no right or wrong way to begin to develop your collection. It's a matter of individual taste.

Naturally, some collectibles cost more than others, so your budget will help you narrow the possibilities (or at least require that you take *time* to collect those items you desire).

Depending on what kind of memorabilia catches your eye, talk with the dealer who is selling that item. If you're unfamiliar with its significance, ask questions. The dealer should know at least a little bit about the item's history or what makes it a unique collectible.

If you notice two items that appear to be alike in every respect but are priced differently, ask the dealer politely why one item is more valuable than the other. The differences may at times be subtle, yet they greatly affect the value the dealer assigns each item.

A classic example of this would be two seemingly identical "Joe Player"-model bats, each signed by Joe in blue Sharpie. One bat sells for $300, the other for $35. The reason? One bat was used by Joe in an actual Major

---

1956
Topps offers a checklist and individual team cards in its set, both of which become industry standards.

1957
Topps manufactures its cards in a new 2½″ × 3½″ size, the format still used today.

When you attend a Major League game, hold on to collectible items you buy at the ballpark: programs, yearbooks, pins, and the like. And keep them in good shape as the years pass. Even if they don't accrue any value on the open market, they will accumulate great importance to you as you get older. They are mementos from a time and place that are part of your personal history.

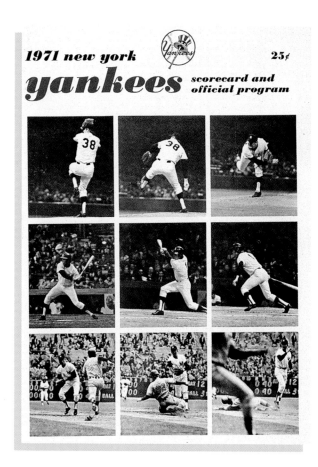

League game, the other was not. (Incidentally, most bat aficionados use specially designed, transparent plastic tubes to carry and store their bats.)

But if bats—game-used and otherwise—are out of *your* league as far as collectibles go, here are some other suggestions as you ponder the wealth of noncard memorabilia available to you:

• official National and American League baseballs, already signed, or blank ones that you can have your favorite player(s) sign for you

• articles from a player's uniform; while jerseys often cost more than bats, such items as caps, leggings, batting gloves, sleeve patches, spikes (cleated shoes), sweatbands, and undershirts, for example, are made available to collectors from time to time at affordable prices

Player uniforms are desirable, expensive collectibles—especially if the uniform was once worn by a Hall of Famer or other big-name star. Always buy uniforms from an established dealer—one who knows the background of the uniforms he is selling and something about their design, numbering, and any special patches.

• vintage pennants (older, original pennants touting the Brooklyn Dodgers, Boston Braves, St. Louis Browns, and so on, or perhaps a series of *your* team's pennants, because the design has probably changed significantly over the years)

• out-of-print reading materials such as classic baseball books, issues of popular sports periodicals such as *Sports Illustrated*, *Baseball Digest*, *The Sporting News*, *Sporting Life* (which predated *TSN*), and team yearbooks, pocket schedules, and media guides

• specially designed plaques of famous ballplayers and managers

• prerecorded videotapes spotlighting selected players, teams, World Series, or eras in the game's history

• ticket stubs and scorecards

- press pins, buttons, and jewelry associated with a particular team or contest (All-Star Game, World Series, and so on)
- table games and children's toys (coin banks, Hartland figurines)
- photographs (black-and-white or color) of famous baseball people.

In a classic rhythm and blues song from 1965, Joe Tex delivers the line "Hold on to what you've got"—and those words fit the concept of collecting any memorabilia, as well. When you go to the ballpark, hold on to that ticket stub, that scorecard, that program you have in your hands.

They are keepsakes that may not mean much to you now because the contest itself is still fresh in your memory. (Plus, your team may even have lost the game.) And keeping them in mint condition—which you should always do—doesn't guarantee they will be valuable to anyone else twenty or even fifty years from now. But in time, they are likely to trigger a lot of memories and emotions in you. As simple as they appear, a ticket stub, a scorecard, or a program will put you back in touch with moments from your personal history. And those moments are something you can share with your family and friends for years to come.

National League umpire Bob Davidson illustrates this point perfectly. Davidson, who worked his first Major League game in 1982 and became a regular member of the NL staff the following year, has his own distinctive collection:

"I save lineup cards of each game I work behind the plate," he explained. "After each game, when I get back to the hotel, I'll turn the card over and on its back I write down the names of the guys I worked with—you know, the umpire at first base, second base, and third base—the score of the game, and I note whether I threw somebody out of the game or if there was some big hoopla.

"I have years' worth of them. I think a lot of umpires are

> **1959**
> Fleer begins issuing (small) sets, the first one an 80-card set spotlighting the life and baseball career of Ted Williams.

Admit it: Displaying your prized possessions is great fun, whether you're 15 or 50. The durable configuration shown here speaks for itself. It looks sharp, honors the player and tells admirers that you are a big fan. And, its design helps protect your collectibles from damage.

doing that kind of very personal collecting these days."

Davidson also collects the occasional autographed baseball. And again, the signatures are of his fellow men in blue. To baseball fans more interested in the players' deeds, this collection would seem OK at best. To Davidson, his unique collection is priceless.

"I have a couple [signed baseballs] from the 1987 All-Star Game," he said, "with the names of all the guys I worked with. That's special to me, because Dick Stello's name is on there. He worked with me, and he was a close friend of mine." (Stello was killed in an automobile accident November 18 of that year, at age fifty-three.)

Granted, a big-league umpire like Bob Davidson has an inside track on such things as umpire-autographed baseballs and lineup cards from actual games, but *you* have the inside track on memorabilia from your own family. Perhaps you or someone else in your family played organized baseball at some level. It doesn't hurt to ask.

One baseball writer who had followed the game since he was seven learned some thirty years later that one of his grandfathers had played semipro baseball in the Chicago area around 1912–1913.

That in itself was a surprise to the writer, but upon further digging he came across his grandfather's catcher's mitt, a baseball dated 1908, newspaper accounts of the team's games over a three-year period, and most important, three mint-condition, black-and-white photographs taken of his grandfather's team. Baseball cards of a sort! So, you may need only to look to your own family to start a collection of baseball memorabilia that is both easy to acquire and personally satisfying.

Beyond that, one of the easiest and least expensive sets of collectibles to obtain is player-autographed photos. Shop around at the hobby shows and conventions, and see if you don't find a terrific selection of pictures of the greats and near-greats, already signed by the individuals themselves.

Dealers have paid the players to autograph the photos (just as they would for them to autograph baseballs, bats, and so forth), and they then offer them to collectors at shows. There is a wide range of prices for these signed mementos. Signatures of Hall of Famers, living or dead, tend to cost a little more than those of other players, as do specially designed prints, plaques, or rare posters, *regardless* of the signer.

Of course, if you want a player (active or retired) to sign the photograph for you in person, you'll need to purchase an unsigned photo prior to the hobby show where he is appearing. An unsigned photo usually goes for just a few bucks, a small price to pay for owning a personalized piece of memorabilia. You can even have the autographed photos framed, if you like, perhaps mounting them in a hallway of your home.

> ### 1961
> Post begins issuing sets of baseball cards printed on the back panels of its breakfast cereal boxes; sets were made until 1964.

One of the more popular collectibles for fans of all ages is also one of our oldest forms of hero worship: autographed baseballs. As with photos, you may purchase a ball already autographed by your favorite player(s) or buy a "blank" one and ask the player to sign it for you in person.

Just remember, whether it's baseball cards or other memorabilia you want to own, half of the fun is in "getting there." There is so much to choose from that you may find yourself obtaining many, many different things for your stash. After all, variety *is* the spice of life—*and* of collecting.

FOLLOWING THE MARKET

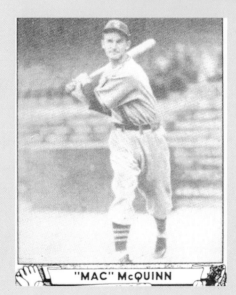

"MAC" McQUINN

"MAC" McQUINN

Another example of the fabled 1940 Play Ball set from Gum Inc. George McQuinn, a 12-year Major League veteran, was the first baseman on the 1944 American League Champion St. Louis Browns. His card (#53) ranges in price from about $7 in good condition to more than $20 in near-mint condition.

For a hobby pursued by millions of people of all ages, it seems strange that no national organization exists to serve the membership. But it has always been this way for those who collect baseball cards and other baseball-related memorabilia. Yet the hobby's network of collectors, dealers, and manufacturers is stronger than at any time in its history. Why? The answer lies in the printed word.

Numerous top-notch publications that serve the hobby provide avid collectors with the kinds of information they need to make wise decisions on buying and selling sports memorabilia. It is through these publications (and through baseball card shows, your local card shop, and weekend hobby conventions) that collectors, dealers, and manufacturers communicate with one another on a large

A distinguishing feature of the Play Ball cards was their detailed player bios on the back. In the stat-driven game of baseball, it's refreshing to look at a card, even an older card, and learn something about the player's contributions, offered in a more humanistic approach.

53. GEORGE HARTLEY McQUINN

First Baseman   St. Louis Browns

Born: Ballston, Va.

Bats: Left   May 29, 1911

Height: 5' 11"   Throws: Left

Weight 170 lbs.

A castoff of the Yankee farm system, George McQuinn proved himself a top-flight first-base-man with the St. Louis Browns. As a hitter, and defensively, McQuinn was one of the outstanding first-basemen in the American League last year. He batted .316, playing in every one of the 154 games for the Browns, drove in 94 runs, scored 101, and hit 20 home runs, 13 triples and 37 doubles. He was tied with Hank Greenberg in fielding with a percentage of .993, making 116 as-sists, more than any other first-sacker and participating in 122 double plays, second only to Babe Dahlgren. The draft brought McQuinn to the Browns from Newark in 1938, and for two successive years he has batted over .300 and collected 195 hits each year.

PLAY BALL

A pictorial news record of America's favorite sport. Save these cards . . . know all about the game and its prominent players. New pictures every year.

© 1940.

GUM, INC., Phila., Pa.

PRINTED IN U. S. A.

REPRINT 1986

scale. Call it "collector bonding."

And whether you're just starting out or you're an advanced collector, there is a wealth of interesting, vital information awaiting you in feature articles, price lists for older and current cards alike, late-breaking hobby news, columns, letters to the editor, listings for upcoming card shows and conventions around the country, and of course, pages and pages of advertisements for virtually every type of baseball collectible under the sun (or under the lights, for that matter).

Some of the publications, such as *Sports Collectors Digest*, have been around for years. Others are relative newcomers. And a few have even changed the publication frequency of their issues, going from twice monthly to weekly and from quarterly to monthly, in response to the

---

1963

Fleer's 66-card set of contemporary players leads to Topps's win in court over the issue of player exclusivity regarding bubble gum cards.

Part of the 1989 Fleer major set, this card pays tribute to the multi-talented Jose Canseco. Although the A's rightfielder is indeed a superstar, with his history-making 40 steals and 42 homeruns, the card itself is not worth as much as others in the 660-card set. The Ken Griffey, Jr. rookie card comes to mind, for one, and the infamous Billy Ripken "obscenity on the bat" card #616d (the third corrected version of #616) is also worth many times more than the depiction of Canseco's admirable accomplishments.

huge appetite that exists for news about baseball cards and collecting.

If you wish to stay informed and entertained, and keep up with the current card prices of players ranging from Doug Jones to Dwight Smith to Ken Griffey, Jr., then help is just a subscription or newsstand visit away:

Sports Collectors Digest
700 East State Street
Iola, Wisconsin 54990

Simply and affectionately known as SCD, this weekly periodical is the hobby's oldest publication. It is also the largest, and you'll get no argument about *that* from U.S. postal employees who try to cram it into thousands and thousands of residential mail slots every week.

It offers in-depth profiles of, and interviews with, current and former athletes, managers and coaches, officials, and sportscasters, as well as of some of the country's most knowledgeable hobbyists and dealers; a "fan reaction" section; news about upcoming sets and subsets (major *and* minor leagues); columns covering various facets of collecting; an updated price guide insert in every issue; and more advertisements than you could possibly read in one sitting. Published by Krause Publications, which, in addition to offering similar hobby periodicals on everything from pop music to stamps to coins, also publishes:

Baseball Cards
700 East State Street
Iola, Wisconsin 54990

Terrific color and black-and-white photos complement the spirited copy in this monthly magazine that somehow manages to retain a great sense of fun about a hobby that its writers and readers take very seriously. This is a good place to learn about baseball's new faces—through BC's feature articles and its free, specially made collector cards inserted in every issue. Also noteworthy is its informative Q & A section.

Baseball Card News
700 East State Street
Iola, Wisconsin 54990

This is the third member of the Krause publications trio of hobby periodicals relating to baseball and other sports. This one is issued twice monthly, and is geared especially to beginning and occasional collectors. Although you can guess its emphasis from its title, BCN also covers collectibles relating to basketball, boxing, football, hockey, and even a few non-sports subjects as well. (To some extent, SCD also gets into those areas.) BCN is geared more toward the beginning collector than is SCD, and thus might be more useful at first.

> ### 1973
> This was the last year Topps issued its major sets in series, thereby making it easier for collectors to complete their sets.

Beckett Baseball Card Monthly
3410 MidCourt, Suite 110
Carrollton, Texas 75006

This popular magazine is named for its founder, Dr. James Beckett, who is still one of the hobby's best friends. (At the 1980 National he received a special award for his contributions to the hobby, the first such award ever presented.) He is also well grounded in the history of baseball and its cards, as evidenced by the articles penned for each issue. Along with his staff, Beckett, who is a professional mathematician and statistician, provides an updated price guide each month. And of course, in every issue readers are given a forum to express their views on the hobby.

Baseball Hobby News
4540 Kearny Villa Road, Suite 215
San Diego, California 92123

Current news, reader comments, feature stories, opinion—it's all here. This monthly tabloid is geared to bring the reader as much usable data and facts as he or she needs to be a well-informed collector. Like any good hobby publication worth its wax pack, BHN reaches beyond baseball cards to include also many other types of baseball collectibles.

Tuff Stuff
Box 1637
Glen Allen, Virginia 23060

As hobby periodicals go, this is one of the new kids on the baseball block. This monthly publication looks at all kinds of sports memorabilia but remains rooted in "cardboard coverage." Whether at the newsstand or through a mail subscription, this is worth seeking out. *Tuff Stuff* is good stuff.

Current Card Prices
P.O. Box 480
East Islip, New York 11730

1974
Topps issues its first "traded" set, which features that year's new rookies as well as traded players in their new uniforms.

Staying abreast of current price changes in the hobby is vital to collectors and dealers nationwide. Publications such as this one also include interesting feature articles about the hobby or the players themselves.

Very popular among card shop owners, dealers, and consumers alike, CCP is a monthly price guide that differs from the Beckett system in that it uses one price (as opposed to Beckett's high/low range) for near-mint or mint cards. CCP covers all the major sets, from the 1948 Bowmans through the most recent issues.

Beginning collectors would do well to make any or all of these publications part of their regular reading. Many already have (and so have thousands of veteran hobbyists).

More advanced collectors should keep the following publications in mind: _Baseball Card Investment Report, The Old Judge,_ and _Guide To Pre-Rookie Prices_ (focusing on hundreds of minor league sets picturing Major League hopefuls). As for books, _Making Money With Baseball Cards_ (Bonus Books), by Paul M. Green and Donn

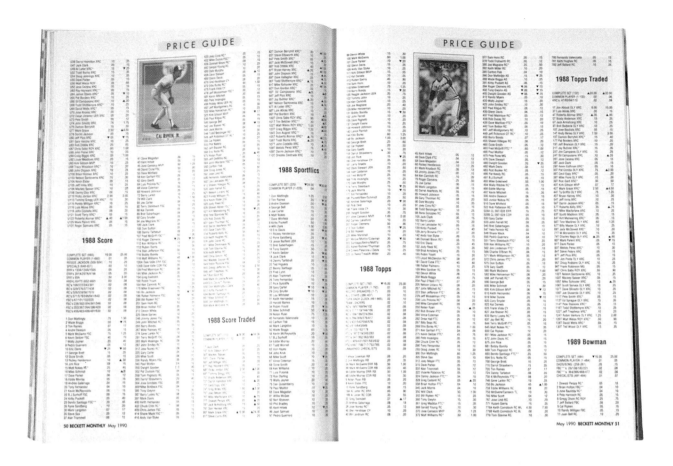

Pearlman, is essential for collectors with an eye toward profit statements.

All are worthwhile publications, to be sure, but not for the squeamish. Beginning collectors who view their purchases as financial investments should check into these publications *after* they have mastered the possibilities. No need to rush things.

There are three softcover books *all* collectors should add to their library: *The Sports Collectors Digest Baseball Price Guide,* from Krause Publications, *The Sport Americana Baseball Card Price Guide,* and Beckett's *The Official Price Guide To Baseball Cards.* Each annual is packed with essential information about card numbers, their varieties, and so forth. Incidentally, with its fourth edition (1990), the SCD price guide began including prices for nearly

1,300 minor league team sets. (Collectors interested in noncard memorabilia should obtain *Beckett's Price Guide To Baseball Collectibles*.)

Most helpful as cross references with other guides are *The Sport Americana Alphabetical Baseball Card Checklist* and *The Sport Americana Baseball Card Team Checklist*. They will help you determine what's available on specific players and teams.

Any hobbyist who also collects autographs should first seek out two inexpensive, softcover books: *The Sport Americana Baseball Address List,* by Jack Smalling and Denny Eckes, and *Collecting Sports Autographs*, by Tom Owens. The first book, updated every two years, provides the mailing addresses of nearly every active and retired Major League player, manager, and umpire since about 1910 (or, the date and place of death, if deceased). It also includes the addresses of big league teams and offers some pointers on obtaining autographs of the people listed in its 150 pages.

Collecting Sports Autographs (from Bonus Books, Chicago) is the hobby's first complete guide to the dos and don'ts of getting athletes' signatures. Owens gives collectors valuable advice on the increasingly popular activity, based on his years of firsthand experience and with input from numerous other collectors around the country. Whether you want to write to famous sports personalities or approach them in person, this book is a must-have for autograph seekers of all ages.

A good way to get more out of your collection is to look into the history of the players and the teams pictured on your baseball cards. While the stats printed on the backs provide you with some of the essential information on the players and managers, they don't tell the whole story. Especially if you own cards of ballplayers "before your time"—even if that time was just a few years ago—it's fun and entertaining to learn about the *people* in those photographs.

Your local lending library is the first place you should

Almost like poring over stock market quotations, isn't it (opposite)? But whether you collect for the investment possibilities or simply to enjoy opening a wax pack to discover what's inside, there's no sin in knowing the market value of something you either own or desire. Price guides—weekly, monthly, and yearly—provide essential information.

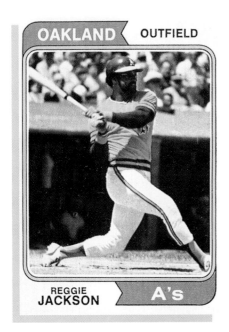

OAKLAND OUTFIELD

REGGIE JACKSON **A's**

"Mr. October"—the moniker that Reggie Jackson would later adopt—is pictured on card #130 in the Topps 1974 majors set. Collectors generally prefer game-action photos of their heroes, and this one of Jackson captures his powerful follow-through.

look to find books on baseball history, because you won't have to pay a cent to use them (unless, of course, you're late in returning them).

Or, if your budget allows and you'd like to buy a baseball book or two, here is just a sampling of entertaining, highly-readable titles you may find helpful. Some are available in less expensive softcover versions, and, by the way, a few of them are chock-full of photographs:

Baseball: The Illustrated History of America's Game, by Donald Honig

Baseball's 50 Greatest Games, published by *The Sporting News*

Baseball's 25 Greatest Pennant Races, published by *The Sporting News*

The Sports Encyclopedia: Baseball, by David S. Neft & Richard M. Cohen

The World Series, by Richard M. Cohen & David S. Neft

The Ultimate Baseball Book, edited by Daniel Okrent & Harris Lewine

The Glory of Their Times, by Lawrence Ritter

The Bill James Historical Baseball Abstract, by Bill James

There are hundreds and hundreds of baseball titles still in print dealing with virtually every aspect of the game's history, such as the Negro Leagues, various team histories, biographies and autobiographies of legendary players and managers, the ballparks of yesterday and today, pre-1900 professional baseball, and of course, the two huge statistical/historical compilations, *The Baseball Encyclopedia* and *Total Baseball*, both of which are updated periodically.

Several books deal directly with the history of baseball cards. Of particular note is *The American Card Catalogue*, compiled by Jefferson R. Burdick. The man dubbed by some "the father of baseball cards" was the hobby's chief historian until his death in 1963. Burdick catalogued cards by year and classification (the "T-206" designation still used today for the tobacco set containing the legendary Honus Wagner card is his). This book, while not a viable price guide in today's market, remains an important cornerstone of the hobby.

There are some worthwhile pictorials to consider, too, including *Classic Baseball Cards: The Golden Years 1886–1956* and *Topps Baseball Cards: The Complete Picture Collection*, both by Frank Slocum. The latter title features annual supplements.

As the 1990s unfolded, of particular interest to speculators in love with rookie cards were such new titles as *Sporting News Top 150 Minor League Prospects* and *Hot Prospects*, which looked at the young players who may be destined for superstardom in the big leagues.

And since this is the video age, you'll be happy to know that a couple of entertaining and informative VHS-format productions made a few years ago are still available to beginning collectors.

An Introduction to Baseball Card Collecting is a thirty-minute overview of hobby basics (grading, pricing, types of sets, and so on) and memorable moments in baseball history hosted by former Major League player Bobby Valentine.

Baseball Card Collector is a sixty-minute video production with celebrated sportscaster Mel Allen as your host. It devotes a significant amount of time to the history of baseball cards. There is a less expensive—and shorter—version of the tape sold at selected stores. But the longer version is the one to have.

So, whether it's periodicals, books, videos, or just talking with fellow collectors, the point is, you'll get so much more from your baseball cards if you connect with the history, the personalities, and the memories those cards represent. After all, what's the point of searching for a hard-to-find "mint" card of Roger Maris if all you know about it is that everybody else seems to want one, too?

Or how about that Mark Fidrych rookie card you bought at a hobby show. Do you know *why* he was called the Bird, or why Detroit Tigers fans appear wistful at the

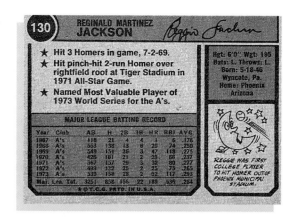

Topps issued its entire 1974 majors set all at once, a departure from what the company had done since 1952: issue cards in series. Topps did issue a traded set late in the summer, however.

1980
The first annual National Sports Collectors Convention is held in Los Angeles; a different city hosts the event each July.

mention of his name, even though his big league career lasted only five seasons? If you get into baseball card collecting only for its possible financial rewards, you're likely to reach burnout before you know it. If the game bores you, then how can you stay with a hobby that glorifies it?

If, on the other hand, you're in love with the game—and follow it on a daily basis and take an interest in its history—the hobby of collecting baseball cards will retain its fascination for you for many seasons to come. Collecting baseball cards, like the game itself, touches the collective soul of America's fans.

Remember: The best fans make the best collectors because the game and the hobby go hand in hand. Or, better still, hand in glove. So, good luck in finding those cardboard keepsakes you want, and have fun!

FUTURE TRENDS

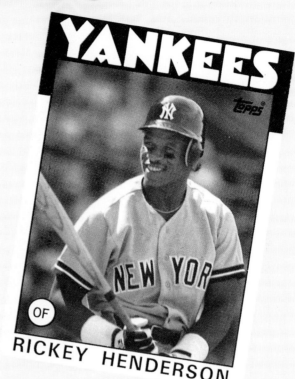

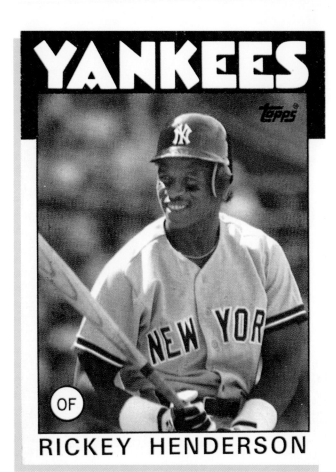

YANKEES

Topps

OF
RICKEY HENDERSON

In a major set, cards of the game's best players are valued higher than are the "commons" in the same set. This Rickey Henderson card from the 1986 Topps set of 792 cards runs about eight times higher than the value of most commons, though that isn't saying a lot since the commons in mint condition run about 5 cents apiece.

Ironically, 1981, the same year that witnessed a maddening two-month player strike that threatened to destroy the entire Major League Baseball season and permanently sour many fans on the National Pastime, also saw a renewed interest in collecting baseball cards and related memorabilia. Since that time, the game of baseball has weathered several other interruptions, including the tragic and disastrous Bay Area earthquake during the 1989 World Series. Somehow, the game has managed to bounce back. And through it all, collecting memorabilia has actually increased in popularity.

Even veteran dealers and other collectors have expressed genuine amazement over their hobby. And though none of them claims to use a crystal ball to see the

Owning modern day cards is like having annual encyclopedias of the individual players. Yearly and career statistics fill the card backs, so collectors can, at a glance, see how a player has performed on the diamond. (Nice goin', Rickey.)

future, here are some thoughts on collecting from several of them:

Bob Lemke, publisher of *Sports Collectors Digest, Baseball Cards* magazine, and other cornerstones of the hobby world:

"I really believe that most of today's collectors can trace their interest in the hobby to a family member a generation back or more. There's a collector mentality, a family tradition type of thing, involved in card collecting. If that's not already in place, chances are collecting won't become a permanent part of your life.

"The hobby is almost at a point now where we've returned to cards being issued in series, the way Topps did until 1974. Some companies are issuing a seemingly endless set of cards anyway, replacing some at midseason

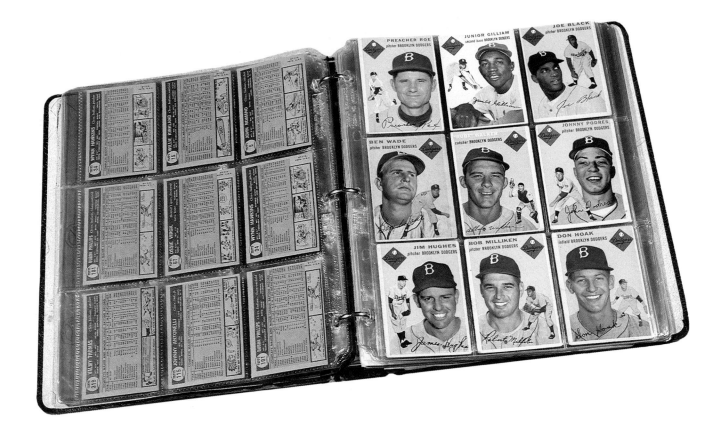

Collecting is personal. You should decide what you want to acquire for your collection. Many hobbyists enjoy owning team sets; that is, the cards of all the players representing a given team in a regular annual (major) set (above). Team sets can be put together one card at a time by the collector, or bought from a dealer who has taken the time to put the sets together for sale to the public.

and things like that. They're almost doing that now with football and basketball cards, and of course, baseball has its traded or updated sets late in the season. But there may be a more obvious effort on the part of the companies to spread their issues out over the course of the season in an attempt to be timely and up-to-date.

"I don't know that we'll see too much more being done with cards—in a technological sense—in the near future. The hobby has pretty well turned its thumbs down on multiple image cards and other stylistic devices. People don't want gimmicks. Having said that, however, I think that we could see more in the area of marketing limited-edition collectibles packaged with cards. That would make buying a pack of cards even more like a lottery than it ever was. But companies will focus on marketing their bread-and-butter items, and move away from doing peripherals such as baseball card books, limited issues, or regional-type presentations. There's virtually too much stuff out there as it is.

"The hobby will remain vibrant and alive for years to come. Even if the serious investors move on to some other area, the hobby has an enormous, grass-roots base of collectors that will continue to keep the hobby alive and active."

Whitie Willenborg, Cincinnati-based dealer, promoter, and collector who, as a teenager, served as an usher at Crosley Field during the 1939 World Series between the Reds and Yankees:

"Every time a kid turns ten years old, it seems, there's always a new ballplayer to idolize…a Mark Grace or a Ken Griffey, Jr. It's a cycle, and it will always be that way. The popularity of a particular player, and how the fans view his successes and failures on the field, will have an impact on the popularity of his baseball cards and other memorabilia.

"Fans can be fickle. One year a guy's a sensation, the next year nobody is looking for his autograph. Sometimes that makes it tough for dealers to determine what they should take to a show.

"As we move into the 1990s, it seems that the big attraction for collectors and fans in general is the superstar or Hall of Famer who's there to sign autographs. That has been a major change in the shows and conventions from what it was several years ago when the cards and memorabilia were what drew people to these events.

"I think baseball cards will remain the staple of the hobby. But, a card may become to the collector what rice is to the Chinese: It will always be a staple and it will always be enjoyed, but there are a lot of other things to enjoy, too. You've got photos, prints, posters, bats and balls, and all kinds of other neat things to consider."

Wanda Marcus, veteran collector, dealer, and hobby show promoter who has twice hosted the National Sports

> ### 1981
> A federal court ruling paves the way for other companies to make baseball cards, and Fleer and Donruss now challenge Topps.

Collectors Convention in Arlington, Texas:

"For the National, the idea in the beginning was to have as guests at least one person from each sport, although I think basketball and hockey players, in particular, have been underrepresented for the most part at major shows and conventions. It is hoped that will change to reflect the growing popularity of their cards. It may be that they will appear at corporate-sponsored booths.

"Baseball cards will continue to be popular with collectors, but the labor problems that troubled the sport throughout the 1980s and into the 1990s turned some fans off. Some of those collectors, and even collectors who still stand by baseball, have turned to football and basketball and hockey cards. The companies have made an effort to issue quality products, and the collectors have responded favorably.

"Even though I'm involved in the buying and selling of sports memorabilia, and promoting shows, I like being part of all this because of the friendships that form from it. Seeing longtime friends and meeting new collectors at these shows around the country—that's what keeps me going. I just love it. I think collecting baseball cards and sports memorabilia is the greatest hobby in America. It *is* fun."

CARD LINGO

Eric Gunderson

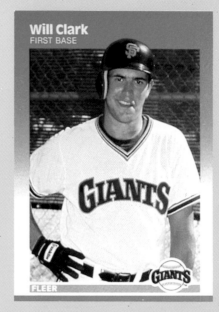

Will Clark
FIRST BASE

FLEER

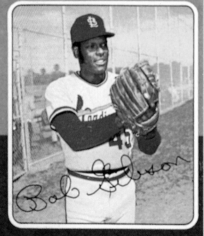

'74 Highlights

GIBSON THROWS 3000th STRIKEOUT

Rookie cards and superstar cards add greatly to a given set. The popularity of such cards among collectors is often a reflection of the players' popularity among all baseball fans.

Baseball has the *6–4–3,* the *worm burner,* and *dial 8.* Do you know what these terms mean? In collecting baseball cards, you've got *collation, wax pack,* and *Panini.* Do you know what *these* terms mean?

In either case, you're likely to get more enjoyment from what you're doing if you understand the words and phrases involved.

What follows is a glossary of basic terms used by collectors, dealers, card manufacturers, and writers that will help you understand the hobby of collecting baseball cards and other memorabilia. Once you've read this glossary a few times, you'll be able to understand card lingo and speak it with the best of them.

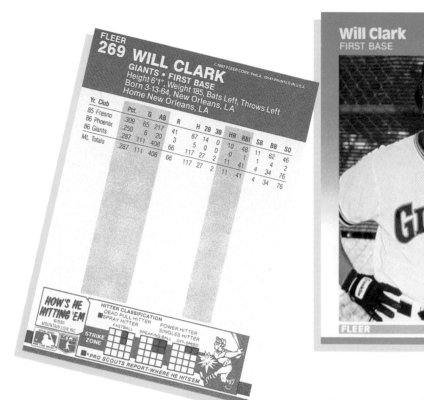

The card shows:

FLEER 269 WILL CLARK
GIANTS • FIRST BASE
©1987 FLEER CORP. PHILA., 19141 PRINTED IN U.S.A.
Height 6'1", Weight 185, Bats Left, Throws Left
Born 3-13-64, New Orleans, LA
Home New Orleans, LA

Yr. Club	Pct.	G	AB	R	H	2B	3B	HR	RBI	SB	BB	SO
85 Fresno	.309	65	217	41	67	14	0	10	48	11	62	46
86 Phoenix	.250	6	20	3	5	0	0	0	1	1	4	2
86 Giants	.287	111	408	66	117	27	2	11	41	4	34	76
ML Totals	.287	111	408	66	117	27	2	11	41	4	34	76

Will Clark
FIRST BASE

Collecting baseball cards like this Will Clark card is as much an American tradition as fireworks on Independence Day and television cartoons on Saturday morning.

ALL-STAR CARD A card identifying a player as a member of a National League, American League, or Major League All-Star team, although the player shown may not necessarily be a member of his league's official All-Star squad for that year. All-Star cards are sometimes issued in special sets, or may be part of a regular set.

ASSORTED Advertising term describing a given lot of cards containing multiples of one or more cards; a lot that does *not* contain multiples is termed *different*.

AUTOGRAPHED CARD (OR BALL, PHOTO, AND SO ON) A card featuring the actual handwritten signature of the player, manager, coach, umpire, or other person shown on that card; auto-

In simpler times collectors would choose from only a few card sets each year. Nowadays, however, in addition to the regular-issue sets and their updated sets, there are regional issues and several new, limited edition sets coming out every year. Some observers see the current situation as a market glut, while others welcome the variety.

graphs can often (but not always) increase the value of the card, but are always preferable to machine-printed facsimile (exact copy) autographs.

BORDER The margin of space, usually white, but different colors are sometimes used, surrounding the picture on the card; among the first things collectors and dealers consider when grading cards are borders.

BOWMAN One of the legendary names in the hobby, this Philadelphia-based company made baseball cards from 1948 to 1955, after which Topps purchased the company and even revived the name in 1989 by issuing a set of "Bowman" cards; Bowman also manufactured football and basketball cards in the 1940s and 1950s.

BOXED SET A set of (usually) thirty-three or forty-four cards issued as a complete set in its own container and sold in discount stores or large retail chain stores; typically, these sets are manufactured by any of the leading companies such as Topps, Fleer, and Donruss and contain only cards of hot rookie players or established stars.

BRICK Cards grouped according to year, team, or other similarity, and sold together.

BUY PRICE What a dealer will pay for specific cards, card sets, or other items, and it's often much lower than the prices listed in the magazines, catalogues, or price guides.

CELLO PACK Cards sold in cellophane-wrapped packages. Despite their higher price tag, these are normally a better buy than wax packs. Cello packs generally feature a wrapping that allows you to see the top and bottom cards, and if either or both of those cards is a hot rookie or established star, the unopened cello pack likely will bring a higher price among collectors.

CENTERING Term referring to the placement of the picture within the card itself; in grading a card, the centering of the picture goes hand in hand with its borders, so a well-centered card is a key element in determining its value.

CHECKLIST Whether printed on a special card within the set itself, or included in hobby publications or price guides, a checklist helps you determine whether you have or don't have one or more cards in the set for modern-era sets especially, checklists arrange the cards in numerical order; unmarked checklist cards within the sets themselves generally are worth more than those that have been marked on.

> **1986**
> Sportflics, with their distinctive "Magic Motion" process, hit the market; multiple images create "movement" in the pictures.

★ ★ ★ **No. 16** ★ ★ ★

Roger Maris

NEW YORK YANKEES — OUTFIELDER

Ht. 6'0"; Wt. 204; Bats Left; Throws Right; Born September 10, 1934; Home: Raytown, Mo. Fans will long remember Roger's feat of 61 HRs in the 1961 season, establishing a record for a 162-game schedule. Named Player of the Year by the Sporting News for 1961 and AL MVP in 1960-61, he led the AL in RBIs (112) in 1960, in 1961 with 142, and received the Gold Glove Award as AL outstanding right fielder in 1960. Roger hit a HR the first time at bat in the 1960 World Series. He has played in 7 All-Star Games.

★ ★ ★ **MAJOR LEAGUE BATTING RECORD** ★ ★ ★

	Games	At Bat	Runs	Hits	2B	3B	HR	RBI	Avg.
1962	157	590	92	151	34	1	33	100	.256
LIFE	842	3053	539	793	117	28	191	557	.260

Post Cereals issued baseball cards from 1960 through 1963, most commonly as the back panels of their cereal boxes. This Roger Maris card is one of the real treasures in the 1963 set. It is valued at well over $100 in near-mint condition.

CHIPPING   In grading lingo, this term refers to colored borders that have been worn away over time.

COIN   Small discs, usually the size of a nickel or a quarter, made of metal or plastic; "coins" are popular with many collectors and typically feature a picture of the player on one side and basic data about him—such as team, position, height, weight—on the other.

CLASSIFYING CARDS   The system of grading cards (mint, near-mint, excellent-mint, excellent, very good, good, fair, and poor) that the hobby uses to determine their condition, which in turn, establishes their value.

COLLATION   To assemble cards in a proper order, usually numerically; sets can be collated by hand or bought already collated by the factory.

COLLECT-A-BOOKS   Multi-page baseball cards made by Impel Marketing, Inc. This new entry into the hobby is the brainchild of former Major League pitcher turned author and entrepreneur, Jim Bouton.

COLLECTOR ISSUE   Card sets that are issued with the collector in mind and not considered part of another set or as a premium to be given away; these sets are often reprinted and occasionally are unauthorized, so normally, they are not a good investment choice; collector issues are sold through hobby dealers.

COMBINATION CARD   A card depicting more than one player, such as teammates and/or brothers, or a father-son tandem that made the big leagues; the phrase is sometimes used interchangeably with "multi-player card."

COMMONS   Cards featuring "common" or "ordinary," players, rather than superstars or hot rookies; the lowest-priced cards in any set or series, commons are easier to acquire than other cards because there is less demand for them.

CREASE   Any type of line, ridge, or mark made by folding or bending a card, and it will substantially lower the grade (and therefore the value) of most cards, unless they are extremely old and/or rare issues.

DECOLLATION   To assemble cards in random order for packaging purposes.

DIE-CUT CARDS   Cards characterized by a "pull-out" section that enables them to stand up, much like a

framed photograph; die-cuts are still issued in limited runs, usually as premium inserts with other cards.

DONRUSS A major card manufacturer that began issuing cards in 1981.

DOUBLE PRINT A card that appears at least twice on the same factory press sheet, making that particular card twice as common as the other cards on the sheet; a card printed less often than other cards in a set is said to be a "short print."

ERROR CARD Any card characterized by one or more mistakes, including misspelled names or words, incorrect statistics, or a picture of one player inadvertently substituted for that of another; error cards usually have no additional value to collectors unless the company issues a corrected version, creating a situation where the error cards—if there are fewer of them—can become more valuable than the corrected cards (see **variations**).

EXTENDED SET A card set issued late in the baseball season to supplement an earlier set.

FACTORY SET A complete card set that the manufacturer has collated, packaged, and (normally) sealed, often with an inner wrap around the cards for added protection; still-sealed factory sets have a higher market value than sets that have been hand-collated.

FLEER A major card manufacturer that first produced baseball cards from 1959 to 1963, then dropped out of sight until 1981, when it resumed production and joined Donruss as Topps's chief competitors in the early 1980s; the company also resumed production of football and basketball cards in the mid-1980s, after a similar hiatus.

FOIL PACK Baseball cards packaged in colorful foil

(Facing page) Autograph hounds adore Hall of Fame postcards because the large format is well-suited to player signatures. Sold by the National Baseball Hall of Fame and Museum in Cooperstown, New York, the postcards feature photo reproductions of the HOF members' plaques.

1988
Score becomes the fourth nationally-distributed baseball card maker in the United States, issuing a well-received 660-card set.

STANLEY FRANK MUSIAL
"THE MAN"

ST. LOUIS CARDINALS 1941-1963 HOLDS MANY NATIONAL LEAGUE RECORDS, AMONG THEM: GAMES PLAYED 3026; AT BAT 10972 TIMES; 3630 HITS; MOST RUNS SCORED 1949; MOST RUNS BATTED IN 1951; TOTAL BASES 6134. LED N.L.IN TOTAL BASES 6 YEARS, SLUGGING PERCENTAGE 6 YEARS. MOST VALUABLE PLAYER 1943-1946-1948. NAMED ON 12 ALL STAR TEAMS. LIFETIME BATTING AVERAGE .331.

NATIONAL BASEBALL HALL OF FAME & MUSEUM
Cooperstown, New York

wrappers; foil packs also come in boxes, most often containing thirty-six packs.

FOOD SET   Cards issued with a food item such as hot dogs, snack chips, or candy, or offered as a mail-in collectible by the food manufacturer.

GLOSS/GLOSSY CARD   For the most part, all baseball cards have a certain degree of surface shine, or gloss, on them, which enhances their desirability and value, but some sets of cards are produced with an extra gloss.

GOUDEY   One of the hobby's legendary card manufacturers, despite the fact that the gum company printed

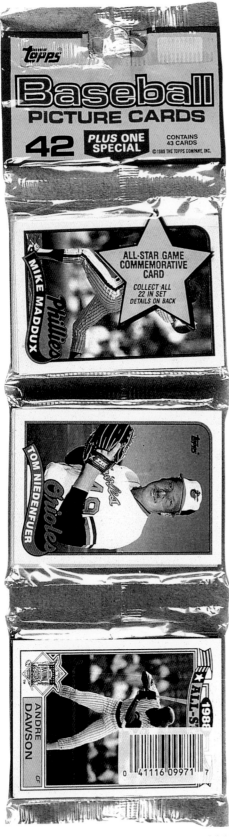

baseball cards for less than a decade (much of the 1930s); it is pronounced "GOO-dee."

GRADE The condition of a card (or other collectible, such as a World Series program or an autographed baseball), which in large part determines its value.

HALL OF FAME POSTCARD Autograph
hounds, particularly, find these oversized cards of baseball's legends desirable because they are well-suited to Hall of Famers' signatures; the cards, which are sold only through the National Baseball Hall of Fame and Museum in Cooperstown, New York, have been issued for decades and are updated periodically with cards of recent inductees; these postcards, which reproduce the member's Hall of Fame plaque, are not to be confused with Hall of Famer *baseball* cards, which are any baseball cards showing a Hall of Famer and usually draw a higher market value than other cards.

HAND-COLLATED SET Any card set assembled
by hand, typically by a dealer, who puts it together one card at a time from wax packs, cello packs, and other sources.

HARTLAND STATUE A high-quality plastic statue
designed and manufactured by the Hartland, Wisconsin–based plastics company from the late 1950s through the early 1960s; Hartland produced and distributed some excellent plastic likenesses of football players, TV western heroes, animals, and other figures during that period, but the company's original eighteen baseball figurines remain, arguably, the most sought after by collectors, not only for the figurines' realistic poses and facial expressions, but for their relative scarcity in mint condition; although the company was bought out in the 1960s and the original molds and design work destroyed, new Hartland baseball statues based on the originals were

issued in the late 1980s by a Texas-based firm.

HIGH NUMBERS   Cards of a particular set that typically were distributed in smaller quantities by the manufacturer, making those cards—even "commons"—very valuable because of their scarcity; through 1973, card makers issued their major sets in series of several hundred cards each, and the later series (containing the high-numbered cards) were not as widely available to collectors because retailers sometimes overbought quantities of the earlier sets, causing inventory problems; the term "high numbers" can also apply to any portion of a set that had a low print run by the manufacturer, regardless of the numbers on those cards.

INSERT   Usually, any collectible (including a sticker, decal, or "coin") included with a pack of cards that serves as a sales gimmick, although inserts can also be packaged with food items as premiums.

KEY CARDS   The most important cards within a set —hot rookies, established superstars, and so forth.

LAYERING   In grading lingo, it's the separation of the layers of paper stock that form the card's thickness; although it most commonly occurs at a card's corners, any type of layering lowers a card's value.

LEAF   The parent company of Donruss, it has also manufactured cards under its own name.

LEGITIMATE ISSUES   Card sets produced to help spur sales of another product or of a particular company; they are frequently sold with food items such as baked goods, candy, or meats, and are not considered collector issues.

LIMITED EDITION   A term used to describe a

See-through cello packs (opposite) are just one way baseball cards are packaged. An unopened cello pack, especially if it shows a hot rookie or an established star such as Andre Dawson, usually commands a higher price than an unopened pack that doesn't.

single item or series with a limited production run, resulting in its relative scarcity; the word *relative* is used here because some limited editions actually enjoy fairly large production runs; regardless of its availability, there is no guarantee that a limited edition *anything* will increase in value over the years.

MAIL-BID AUCTION A type of auction in which collectors send in their bids on items; the highest bidder gets the goods.

MAJOR SET As the words imply, any large set produced by one of the major card makers and distributed nationwide.

MEGALOT A term describing a large group of cards of a specific player, such as the Don Mattingly rookie card, purchased as an investment.

MINI SETS Smaller-size cards that can be either reproductions of existing cards or distinct cards in their own right.

MISCUT A card of little or no value because it has been incorrectly cut at the manufacturing plant; examples of a miscut include a card with a player's picture well off-center or a card with portions of two players' pictures on it.

MOTHER'S Although not considered a BMOC (big maker of cards) this cookie company headquartered in northern California has been offering sets of very popular, high-gloss baseball cards since the early 1980s.

NOTCHING A grading term indicating indentations on a card, often the result of a rubber band being looped around a stack of cards; "rubber bands" should not be part of any collector's vocabulary.

1989
Upper Deck joins the ranks as the fifth national baseball card company with its colorful (and popular) 700-card set.

—7—
Doyle

This card is an example of a player from the California League (later the Pacific Coast League) considered to be some of the most scarce of all Old Judges. The pose itself differs from most Old Judge poses in that the photo is taken outdoors, whereas the great majority of Old Judge photos are studio shots. You can also note that the card does not contain a copyright date, a peculiarity of all California League Old Judge cards.

This is one of 20 cards in SERIES 1 of the Old Judge type set REPRINT series.

DOYLE, 3rd B., San Fran's
OLD JUDGE
CIGARETTE FACTORY.
GOODWIN & CO., New York.

Reprint cards, such as this one from an Old Judge tobacco issue of the late 19th century, may offer a little bit of history about the set itself. (Aw, c'mon, Mr. Doyle, show some enthusiasm, will ya?)

OLD JUDGE A brand of late-nineteenth-century cigarettes that for four years issued baseball cards as an inducement to buy the cigarettes.

O-PEE-CHEE The Topps company's Canadian licensee, it manufactures sets of sports cards featuring bilingual (French and English) backs.

OUT OF REGISTER Printing term describing what happens when the various colors used in a card's photograph are not aligned properly (example: the blue of a player's cap "bleeds" beyond the outline of the cap and onto his face); a picture that is out of register lowers a card's value.

Baseball Extra

③ ST. LOUIS, MO., — JULY 17, 1974

BOB GIBSON ACHIEVES 3000 CAREER STRIKEOUTS

Tonight, Bob Gibson became the first National League pitcher to break the 3000 career Strikeout barrier. Cincinnati's Cesar Geron- imo was his 3000th victim. Walter Johnson holds the lifetime mark of 3,508 Strikeouts and Bob is second on all- time list.

*© 1975 TOPPS CHEWING GUM, INC. PRTD IN U.S.A.

Topps' 1975 set led off with seven consecutive specialty cards high- lighting the previous season's achievements of several ballplayers. Card #3 is a recap of hard-throwing Bob Gibson's three-thousandth career strikeout.

P.O.R. Abbreviation for "price on request."

PANINI A firm that manufactures popular sports stickers.

PEREZ-STEELE The name of a Pennsylvania-based operation that produces artistic renderings of Hall of Famers and other baseball stars on cards that are very popular with collectors.

POLICE SETS Typically, a special card set made on behalf of a local police department as a "freebie" to give to youngsters; a key ingredient of many of these sets is a message on the cards warning against the dangers of drug use or promoting safety in the home; local fire departments also distribute specially made card sets with their own safety messages directed at kids.

POST CEREALS In the hobby world, this breakfast food company is best-known for its baseball and football cards, which it printed on the back panels of its cereal boxes during the early 1960s; most kids back then cut out each individual card, but the more valuable Post collect- ibles are the entire panels of cards left uncut; more than twenty-five years after it ceased producing cards, the company began issuing new baseball cards as cereal box inserts.

PROMO (PROMOTIONAL) CARDS Simply, a card made to promote a product, service, or even a par- ticular card set; usually, "promos" have limited press runs and distribution, which makes them highly desirable to collectors; they are not always available to the public.

PROOF CARDS/PROOF STRIPS Cards or strips of cards not intended for sale to the general public but used by the manufacturer to see that the cards' color registration, statistical data, and so on, are correct before the cards are mass-produced.

RACK PACK   Any number of cards that are usually, but not always, placed in three sections in one long package and which are wrapped in cellophane and displayed on pegboard at retail outlets; a rack *box* holds approximately two dozen rack packs.

RARE   The term describing a card or other collectible item that is limited in quantity and therefore very valuable.

REGIONAL SET   A card set distributed in a specific geographical area of the country, often focusing on a specific team.

REPRINT   A card or set of cards that, as the saying goes, is "brought back by popular demand" because of scarcity of the original; less valuable than the original item, reprints should be designated as such on their packaging.

ROOKIE CARD   An athlete's first card by a major manufacturer in a mass-marketed set available to the general public, even if the card is not actually issued in the player's rookie season; some cards of this type actually have more than one rookie player pictured, yet if even one of the players winds up in the Hall of Fame or at least has a solid Major League career, that card's value will increase substantially over time.

SASE   Abbreviation for self-addressed, stamped envelope.

SCARCE   A card or other collectible that is tough to find and expensive to buy; used interchangeably with the word "rare."

SCORE   The brand name of baseball cards from Major

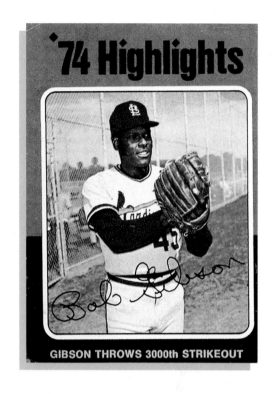

'74 Highlights

GIBSON THROWS 3000th STRIKEOUT

Legendary Cardinals ace Bob Gibson may have smiled for the photographer who shot this picture, but in a game situation "Hoot" was more prone to glaring and growling. A player's facsimile signature isn't likely to affect a card's value one way or the other since it is part of the manufacturer's design. But collectors differ on the merits of having an actual signature on the card; some view it as a plus, while others consider it to be a type of defacement.

Special cards, such as the one pictured here, can help liven up a card set. Cards of this kind may spotlight the league leaders in certain statistical categories, All-Star selections, or pennant winners. This 1970 Topps entry—called a ''team card''—shows the previous year's American League Champions on the front side, and selected historical data on the back side—including the franchises's earlier successes (and stars) in St. Louis.

1990
The hobby of collecting baseball cards and related memorabilia, now in its second century, is at an all-time high in popularity.

League Marketing; noteworthy for their full-color backs, they first appeared in 1988 (see **Sportflics**).

SELL PRICE The price at which a card dealer will sell cards, usually much higher than his or her buy price.

SERIES This term usually applies to the Topps baseball card sets issued from 1952 to 1973; it refers to the manner in which those sets were distributed: several series of cards, numerically ordered, made up a complete set; since 1974, Topps has issued its complete major sets at one time (see **High Numbers**).

SET The complete run of cards in a given issue, anywhere from just a few cards in a specialty or a regional set to the 600 to 800 cards found in the major sets released each year.

SPECIAL CARDS Those cards portraying something other than an individual player, such as National League All-Star, American League champions or, league leaders in RBIs, home runs, ERA, and so forth.

SPORTFLICS The brand name of Major League Marketing's unique multi-image baseball cards, first issued in 1986 (see **Score**).

STAR CARD Any card spotlighting a player who, generally, is considered better than average but slightly below "superstar" status.

STARTER SET An incomplete card set created for beginning collectors with the idea that they will eventually complete the set; starter sets come in various forms, and are sometimes offered via mass media such as television commercials and magazine ads.

STARTING LINEUP The name of both a line of

plastic figurines with accompanying baseball cards produced by Kenner Toys and of a computer baseball game from Parker Brothers that incorporates baseball cards.

STOCK
The cardboard that manufacturers use to make baseball cards.

SUPERSTAR CARDS
A reference to those cards featuring the game's best players, past and present.

TEAM CARD
A card with a group photo of a particular team.

TEAM SET
A term describing all the cards of a given set picturing members of one team; for example, the cards of Oakland's Mark McGwire, Jose Canseco, Dennis Eck-

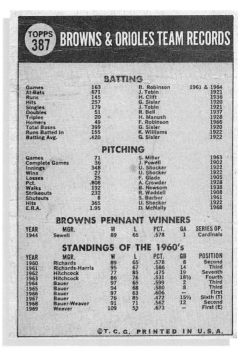

ersley, Dave Henderson, Rickey Henderson, and others, from the 1990 Donruss set; hobby dealers differ in their definitions of "team set," so some dealers elect not to include a team's rated rookies and offensive and defensive leaders—you would likely have to buy those cards separately; if in doubt, ask the dealer which cards/players are included before you buy a team set.

TEAM-ISSUED SET As the term implies, a card set issued by a team, either as a giveaway at the ballpark or as a retail item.

TINS A term for special glossy sets packaged in eye-catching tin boxes.

TOBACCO CARDS Cards printed in the late nineteenth century and early twentieth century as premiums with cigarettes or other tobacco products; even in less than mint condition, some tobacco cards are among the hobby's most pricey collectibles.

TOPPS Issuer of full-color baseball cards since 1952.

TRADED SETS Also known as update sets, these are special sets issued near season's end to reflect the trades that occurred after the regular, larger sets were issued months earlier; they typically also include rookies not spotlighted in the regular sets.

UPPER DECK Nearly 100 years after the introduction of tobacco cards, this manufacturing newcomer from southern California began issuing high-quality baseball cards in 1989 that are noteworthy for their photography.

VARIATION Two, and sometimes more, versions of the same card, often the result of an error contained in the first card that was issued; the value of variations depends greatly on the quantities issued of the original

Upper deck debuted in 1989 with a major set that was well-received by the hobby world. The company joined Donruss, Fleer, Score, and Topps to become one of the "Big Five" baseball card companies.

Eric Gunderson

card and of its successors (see **error card**); the best-known recent example of this situation is the infamous Billy Ripkin "obscenity card."

WAX PACK The cornerstone of retail packaging as far as baseball cards go, a wax pack is a fixed number of cards (averaging between 10 and 15, depending on the manufacturer), sealed in a wax wrapper and packaged with such premiums as bubble gum (a Topps exclusive), a sticker, or puzzle pieces; unopened wax packs present the collector with an interesting dilemma, as they may or may not contain valuable cards; also, cards that come in contact with the wrapper sometimes get stained by the wax, and that lowers the value of those cards.

WRONG BACK A form of "error" card, wrong backs picture one player on the front, with the stats and personal info of another player on the back.

INDEX